ie M.,
services in

VOYA Guides

eries Editor: Cathi Dunn MacRae

Designed for library professionals who work with teens, the VOYA Guides book series expresses the mission of the magazine, *Voice of Youth Advocates* (*VOYA*), to promote youth participation, advocacy, and access to information.

These lively, practical VOYA Guide handbooks:

- Showcase innovative approaches to the youth services field
- Cover varied topics from networking to programming to teen self-expression
- Share project ideas that really work with teens
- Reflect the real world of the library, classroom, or other spaces where teens gather
- Focus on adult mentoring and advocacy of teens
- Feature teen voices and input
- Target librarians, educators, and other professionals who work with teens

1. *Teen Volunteer Services in Libraries*, by Kellie M. Gillespie, 2004

Teen Volunteer Services in Libraries

Kellie M. Gillespie

VOYA Guides, No. 1

VOYA Books
An Imprint of
The Scarecrow Press, Inc.
Lanham, Maryland, and London
2004

VOYA Books
An Imprint of Scarecrow Press, Inc.

Published in the United States of America
by Scarecrow Press, Inc.
A wholly owned subsidiary of The Rowman & Littlefield Publishing Group, Inc.
4501 Forbes Boulevard, Suite 200, Lanham, Maryland 20706
www.scarecrowpress.com

PO Box 317
Oxford
OX2 9RU, UK

British Library Cataloguing in Publication Information Available

Library of Congress Cataloging-in-Publication Data

Gillespie, Kellie M., 1960–
    Teen volunteer services in libraries / Kellie M. Gillespie.
        p. cm.—(VOYA guides series ; no. 1)
    Includes bibliographical references and index.
    ISBN 0–8108–4837–6 (pbk. : alk. paper)
  1. Teenage volunteer workers in libraries. 2. Teenage volunteer
workers in libraries—United States—Case studies. I. Title. II.
Series.
Z682.4.V64 G55 2004
021.2—dc22

                                        2003017932

CONTENTS

Contents

FORMS AND ILLUSTRATIONS

ACKNOWLEDGMENTS

As many librarians know, the field of young adult services has always relied upon a network of people sharing ideas and encouragement. This book is no different. Many who work with teen volunteers in libraries all across the country have graciously contributed to this manual. I cannot thank them enough for their wisdom, advice, enthusiasm, creativity, and patience.

CONTRIBUTORS:
Hope Baugh, Carmel Clay Public Library, Carmel, Indiana
Chris Carlson, *VOYA* Advisory Board, St. Charles, Illinois
Jeanette Cohn, Rockaway Township Free Public Library, Rockaway, New Jersey
Yvonne K. Coleman, Winchester Public Library, Winchester, Massachusetts
Julie Dahlen, Paso Robles Public Library, Paso Robles, California
Jane R. Deacle, Wake Forest Public Library, Wake Forest, North Carolina
Janice Gennevois, City of Mesa Library, Mesa, Arizona
Francisca Goldsmith, Berkeley Public Library, Berkeley, California
Kristi L. Hanson, Salina Public Library, Salina, Kansas
Mary McKinney, Tucson-Pima Public Library, Tucson, Arizona
Kimberly Paone, Elizabeth Public Library, Elizabeth, New Jersey
Marita Richards, Allen Public Library, Allen, Texas
Stacy Schimschat, Waco-McLennan County Library, Waco, Texas
Diane Tuccillo, City of Mesa Library, Mesa, Arizona
Rebecca Van Dan, Middleton Public Library, Middleton, Wisconsin
Katherine Wanderer, Fairfax County Public Library, Fairfax, Virginia
Karen Wendt, Monona Public Library, Monona, Wisconsin
Sydna Wexler, Broward Public Library, Fort Lauderdale, Florida

I also owe a big thanks to Cathi Dunn MacRae for her guidance and patience during the whole book writing and editing process. As my agitation increased in direct proportion to the book's approaching deadline, she answered each frantic e-mail with attentive detail and calming reassurance. Likewise, I must thank my colleagues at the City of Mesa Public Library who listened to my writing woes, offered thoughtful advice, and worked my desk hours so I could take some time off to finish. I can't forget to mention my four children, Christian, Sarah, Elijah, and Jonah, who prepared me so well for working with teens. And lastly, I owe not only thanks but a month's worth of homemade dinners and chocolate chip cookies to my husband, Joe, who never complained when I had to work and supported me with neck rubs, clean laundry, and words of encouragement whenever they were needed.

INTRODUCTION

When I graduated from library school in 1991, most of us had never heard of the Internet, database searching was very expensive and not available to most small libraries, and I was scared to death to start my first professional position as a children's librarian in southern New Jersey. Although I had taken many classes pertaining to youth services, I had no idea how to do the practical things associated with being a librarian—like ordering books or setting up a summer reading program. There was no one to show me, no listservs to consult, no mentors to ask. Eventually I learned how to do these things and more, but it took a lot of trial and error—mostly error—before programs and services settled into a routine.

I kept thinking about this feeling of inexperience as I wrote this guide, so I tried to include practical information intended for anyone who wants to offer a volunteer program for teens but has no idea how to start. It's also intended for library staff who have some experience with teens or programming, but need some direction or support to begin a volunteer program. Even if a young adult librarian knows everything there is to know about teen programs, services, and teenagers in general, this guide might serve to generate some ideas or help solve a problem. I hope this book provides guidance and help to library staff looking for answers, whether new to library services, or just new to working with teen volunteers.

I have tried to include every aspect of teens' volunteering in libraries, including the special circumstances of school media centers, service learning, and court-ordered community service. I have not included internships or employment for teens in which they receive financial reward. When money is involved, the focus of the program changes and different values emerge to reflect this "payment for work" dynamic. While I would hope that supervisors would still reward teens with special recognition events and evaluate them according to the guidelines developed for any employee whether paid or volunteer, internships and similar programs attract teens interested in making money and not necessarily because of many other reasons teens often volunteer. It does not make the information in this book unhelpful; however, it does cause some aspects, like motivation and recognition, to be somewhat irrelevant when money is involved. I have also limited the scope of this guide to teen volunteer programs that take place in a library setting. There are two forthcoming VOYA Guides that cover other teen volunteer programs that might be of interest to professionals working with teens: *Library Teen Advisory Groups* by Diane Tuccillo and *Give 'Em What They Want: Library Programming for Teens* by Kevin King. I am proud to be a part of this effort and hope that my contribution helps support and encourage teens to embrace volunteerism and community involvement long into their adult lives.

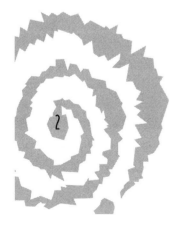

Why Teens as Volunteers?

Teenagers have always been hard to define, but today's teens are more difficult than ever to pin down. Who are they and what do they want? Ask ten different adults about today's teenagers and receive ten different answers. Teens themselves don't make it any easier—each one is determined to express his or her own identity in a unique way. They come in all shapes, sizes, and colors. They wear baggy pants, tight jeans, T-shirts with profanity or teddy bears, jewelry everywhere on their bodies, spiked purple hair or no hair at all. Ask a teen and he or she is too thin, too fat, too tall, too short, not good-looking enough, unpopular, or has lots of friends. Some have great self-images; some can't think of one single thing to like about themselves. They hate being categorized but often label their classmates according to appearance, academic performance, or hobbies. Freaks, cowboys, brains, or jocks—the labels were around when I was a teenager, and they are still around today—only there are more of them. My son recently informed me that in his school there are geeks, nerds, skaters, goths, wannabes, gangsters, cheerleaders, and, of course, jocks.

Our perceptions about today's teens are right on the money. According to the survey document, "2001–2002 State of Our Nation's Youth," American teenagers are more diverse than ever. "Attempts at narrow classification would be a disservice to the youth of America, who come from varied circumstances and are heading in more different directions than ever before."[1] They are more racially and ethnically diverse than adults and also have very different interests and home lives. In addition, they demonstrate such varied approaches to their academics, their challenges, and their plans for the future, that it is difficult to generalize about the current generation. However, the study reveals many interesting facts and a few surprises about today's teenagers that may prove helpful or have a negative impact on their commitment to volunteer service.

Many teens are involved in extracurricular activities; 85% participate in at least one and 49% participate in at least two or more. Seventy-four percent plan to attend college after high school, and 57% expect that scholarships will pay for at least part of their college education. Nearly half (43%) of those surveyed hold paying jobs—and of those, 59% are high school juniors and 60% are seniors. How do they see volunteer service? Forty-nine percent of those who plan to attend college believe it is important to make a contribution to society in order to succeed in life. In fact, teens today define success differently than we might think. "When asked to look ahead and

OUR NATION'S YOUTH
"Life for today's high school students may not be simple or easy, but this year's State of Our Nation's Youth survey shows that they see far more right than wrong in their lives. They may not live in traditional families, but they feel they can count on their families for support. They may not always feel safe in school, but they know that their teachers and administrators care about their concerns. They realize the challenge of paying for college, but believe in its importance and plan on continuing their education after high school. They have problems, but refuse to let them interfere with their lives. They feel pressured for time, but find time for their studies. They care about success, but define success in terms of relationships and contributions, not money or fame."[2]

PRESSURES TEENS FACE		
	Problem	Not a Problem
Pressure to get good grades	62%	38%
Pressure to look a certain way	46%	53%
Family pressures	46%	54%
Financial pressures	42%	57%
Pressure to do drugs or drink	36%	64%
Loneliness or feeling left out	33%	67%
Pressure to have sex	30%	69%
2001–2002 State of Our Nation's Youth[5]		

think about their personal definition of success, most of today's youth say that having close family relationships is very important to them. Similarly, many teenagers say that having a close group of friends will be an important measurement in gauging their success in life. Traditional definitions of success, such as making money and being famous, are less important to this generation of Americans."[3]

These observations do not mean that today's teens don't have problems, as indicated by current events in the news. School shootings, drug and alcohol abuse, suicide, car accidents, and sexual and physical abuse—newspapers document horrific things done by and to young adults almost every day. Some of it is accidental, some not. According to a recent report, "America's Children: Key National Indicators of Well Being 2002,"[4] three out of every four adolescents age fifteen to nineteen die due to injury, including homicide, suicide, and unintentional injuries. Children age twelve to seventeen are twice as likely as adults to be victims of serious violent crimes. In 2000, 19 percent of all serious crimes involving juveniles involved a juvenile offender. The statistics involving teen drinking and illicit drug use are scarcely more optimistic, even though this percentage has been steadily declining in recent years. In 2001, 25% of all tenth graders reported that they had a heavy drinking episode in the last two weeks, and 23% had used illicit drugs in the last thirty days. These numbers are not very encouraging. In fact, they cause some people to avoid teenagers, even to fear them. So, why should we bother even developing programs to serve them?

Those of us who serve teens want to do so because the majority of them are great people. We know that because we live with them, we work with them, and most of all, we love them. We remember that we used to be just like them. We know that teens try to act cool because they are insecure about themselves and worried about finding their way in life. We remember that teens need a place to belong and they want to feel as if they can make a difference in the world. Unfortunately, those of us who strive to provide opportunities for young adult services in our libraries don't control the funding for these programs. Indeed, there are many library administrators and board members who believe that today's teenagers are not worth the time, money, and energy that is required to provide the kinds of library programs that serve this segment of the population. And since teens are their own worst advocates, this attitude won't change unless parents, teachers, librarians, and community leaders speak up for them.

JUSTIFYING A TEEN VOLUNTEER PROGRAM

Libraries are service institutions. This is a good thing because any kind of library volunteer program requires a lot of work from paid staff. Teen volunteer programs require even more energy, time, and effort than adult volunteer programs. Any justification of a teen volunteer program must include an emphasis on serving teens. Trying

4

to sell a teen volunteer program as a way to save time for the paid staff is misleading and unfair to the teens and the staff.

Many volunteer programs cater to adults and their many skills and abilities. These programs are extremely beneficial to the library in a variety of ways. Adults who volunteer can expand library services by doing routine tasks and special projects, thereby freeing up staff to work on more ambitious and complicated projects. Sometimes they have specialized skills that lend themselves to specific needs of the library, such as computer hardware or graphic art design. When volunteers can support staff by doing tasks or add their knowledge to supplement other services, the benefit of using volunteers is easily justified by figuring time saved for staff and expanded services for library users.

Using teen volunteers, however, does not ultimately free staff to pursue other tasks, nor do teens usually bring added skills to the library. There are always exceptions, but in most cases, library staff must spend a great deal of extra time to train teens to do each task assigned. These tasks are still essential and important, but the time involved with hiring, training, evaluating, motivating, and defending the need to employ them as volunteers is much, much more than the value assigned to their completed duties. Teen volunteer programs are not about us. They are not about how much teens can do for library staff, library funding, or library resources. Teen volunteer programs are about the teens. These kinds of programs can only be viewed as services libraries provide to teens and for teens, like story times for preschoolers, homework help for school children, or book discussion groups for senior citizens. And just like those other programs, programs for teens take a lot of time, money, energy, and commitment.

So how on earth do we justify having a teen volunteer program? First, we emphasize the benefits to the participating teens. They learn valuable working skills that often transfer to paying jobs later on. They acquire customer service experience and learn how to interact with a variety of people. They learn the importance of speaking and dressing appropriately and the meaning of dependability and responsibility—often foreign concepts to teens who have no guidance or demands placed upon them. They learn that if they don't perform to certain levels, there are consequences to their actions. They also learn that libraries are welcoming places that have much to offer them. Many teens have never been to their local library and have no idea that there are books, music CDs, videos, DVDs, and programs just for them. In addition, they learn about serving others and how rewarding it can be to give something back to their community. All these things help them develop positive feelings of self-worth and personal achievement as they successfully complete projects and help others.

Another benefit for the teens is the "credit" they receive for volunteering. Many schools have community service hours that are required of their students. Although

> **ADOLESCENT VOLUNTEER STATISTICS**
> - 55% of teens in grades nine to twelve participated in volunteer activities in 1999 (up from 50% in 1996)
> - Regular participation in volunteer activities for 35 or more hours of activities during the school year is associated with higher levels of political knowledge and interest and confidence in public speaking.
> - Girls are more likely than boys to volunteer. In 1999, 57% of girls in grades six to twelve volunteered as opposed to 47% of boys.
> - Students with more highly educated parents are more likely to participate in volunteer activities: 65% of students in grades six to twelve had parents who attended grad school, and 37% had parents with no high school diploma.
> - Students are more likely to volunteer if their schools require and arrange service—59% as opposed to 29% who attended schools with no such requirement.
> *America's Children 2000*[6]

some may argue that this system is coercing teens into volunteer work, I firmly believe that some young adults need a little pushing to try new things. The required hours are usually minimal. Teens can use this opportunity to experience different kinds of work. If they don't like the organization or if the work doesn't appeal to them, they can try something else. Often, however, teens find that they enjoy volunteering, and continue doing it longer than the minimum time required. This commitment leads to another positive outcome from volunteering—college applications and scholarships. As a parent of a high school senior, I can testify to the number of college scholarships that require volunteer service. Libraries are a great place to get that experience. It looks good on college essays, too.

Clearly teens can benefit from their volunteer experiences. But what about the benefits to the library and its staff? To justify this kind of programming, it is helpful to emphasize the intangible benefits that can result from teens' volunteering in the library. First of all, teens add to the diverse population of a library community. They are an important segment of our population and we need to include them so that we are complete as a library community. Secondly, not only is it important for teens to have positive experiences with libraries, it is important for library staff and the public to have positive interactions with teenagers. When a teen helps an adult who is not computer-savvy navigate the Internet, it leaves the library user with a positive impression of teenagers in general. When a staff member sees a teen volunteer cheerfully shelve picture books while talking to kids about fun books to read, then that staff person can see the value of their work in the library. As youth workers, we know the value of each and every teen. If teens have more visibility in our libraries and in our communities, maybe more adults will appreciate them, too.

Another benefit of teens' working as library volunteers is the feedback they can provide to young adult staff trying to maintain current materials in the collection. I was watching a rather painful exchange between a librarian and a young adult recently. The teen was trying to find out if the library had a music CD by a certain band that is currently popular. The librarian had absolutely no idea what the girl was talking about.

"Do you have any Cake?" Teen Girl asked Librarian.

"Cake?" Librarian repeated, obviously puzzled.

"Yeah, Cake. Do you have any?"

"Do you want to know how to make cake? I can show you the cookbooks."

"No! Cake! You know, 'Short Skirt, Long Jacket!'" Teen Girl rolls her eyes.

Librarian, totally lost, looks to me for help. I take pity on her and explain that Cake is the name of a popular band. Yes, the library owns several music CDs by this band. Score: Teen Girl: 1, Librarian: 0. Don't let this happen to you.

It is okay to pick the brains of the teens hanging around your library. It is even better if they are volunteers and available for this task on a regular basis. Believe me, they will absolutely love giving input into the movies, music, and books that should be purchased for the teen collections. This teen input is essential for collection development. As "cool" YA librarians, we might think that we can keep current by reading *YM*, watching *MTV*, and checking out the recent releases at Blockbuster's, but it does not always work. According to the media, Britney Spears is really hot with teens right now, so we might buy all the music CDs and books about her that we can find. Then we find out (usually when we're bragging about keeping up with current teen tastes), that only "babies" like Britney Spears. And we further hear that this is a "lame library," with a "bunch of old stuff for little kids." Ouch! By talking to our teen volunteers, we can keep current with popular trends in musicians, movie stars, movies, and fashion. But don't talk to just one—teens are as different as adults and have a variety of tastes. And this input, to me, is one of the most valuable ways teens can benefit the library.

NOTES

1. "2001–2002 State of Our Nation's Youth," Horatio Alger Association of Distinguished Americans, 2002, www.horatioalger.com/pubmat/submit01.cfm (10 Aug. 2002), 11.
2. "2001–2002 State of Our Nation's Youth," 14.
3. "2001–2002 State of Our Nation's Youth," 10.
4. "America's Children: Key National Indicators of Well Being 2002," America's Children 2002, www.childstats.gov/ac2002/pdf/health.pdf (15 Aug. 2002), 10.
5. "2001–2002 State of Our Nation's Youth," 3.
6. "Youth Participation in Volunteer Activities," America's Children 2000, www.childstats.gov/ac2000/spectxt.asp#spec2 (15 Aug. 2002).

2 Getting Started

It seems that every volunteer guidebook emphasizes the importance of evaluating the needs of the library when setting up a volunteer program. This *is* important—for programs that focus on adults. However, when setting up teen volunteer programs, the emphasis is on the teens. The questions to ask are: what are the needs of the teens in the community, and how can the library meet those needs with a volunteer program? Before answering these questions, however, it is important to examine the different stages of adolescent development to understand fully what motivates teens to volunteer.

ADOLESCENT DEVELOPMENT

All of us who work with young adults have a basic understanding of child and adolescent development. Some of it was learned from formal education classes and some from experience. After all, we were once teenagers ourselves, and even with selective amnesia, we can pretty much remember most of the gory details. Since the physical, emotional, and social changes are so central to working with teens, I have included a brief outline of the two main stages of normal adolescent development, as defined by the American Academy of Child and Adolescent Psychiatry.

MIDDLE SCHOOL AND HIGH SCHOOL YEARS

Movement Toward Independence
- Struggle with sense of identity
- Feeling awkward or strange about one's self and one's body
- Focus on self, alternating between high expectations and poor self-concept
- Interests and clothing style influenced by peer group
- Moodiness
- Improved ability to use speech to express one's self
- Realization that parents are not perfect; identification of their faults
- Less overt affection shown to parents, with occasional rudeness
- Complaints that parents interfere with independence
- Tendency to return to childish behavior, particularly when stressed

Future Interests and Cognitive Changes

- Mostly interested in present, limited thoughts of future
- Intellectual interests expand and gain in importance
- Greater ability to do work (physical, mental, emotional)

Sexuality

- Display shyness, blushing, and modesty
- Girls develop physically sooner than boys
- Increased interest in the opposite sex
- Movement toward heterosexuality with fears of homosexuality
- Concerns regarding physical and sexual attractiveness to others
- Frequently changing relationships
- Worries about being normal

Morals, Values, and Self-Direction

- Rule and limit testing
- Capacity for abstract thought
- Development of ideals and selection of role models
- More consistent evidence of conscience
- Experimentation with sex and drugs (cigarettes, alcohol, and marijuana)[1]

LATE HIGH SCHOOL YEARS

Movement Toward Independence

- Increased independent functioning
- Firmer and more cohesive sense of identity
- Examination of inner experiences
- Ability to think ideas through
- Conflict with parents begins to decrease
- Increased ability for delayed gratification and compromise
- Increased emotional stability
- Increased concern for others
- Increased self-reliance
- Peer relationships remain important and take an appropriate place among other interests

Future Interests and Cognitive Changes

- Work habits become more defined
- Increased concern for the future
- More importance is placed on one's role in life

Sexuality

- Feelings of love and passion
- Development of more serious relationships
- Firmer sense of sexual identity
- Increased capacity for tender and sensual love

Morals, Values, and Self-Direction

- Greater capacity for setting goals
- Interest in moral reasoning
- Capacity to use insight
- Increased emphasis on personal dignity and self-esteem
- Social and cultural traditions regain some of their previous importance[2]

TEENS' NEEDS

We know the benefits of having a teen volunteer program. We know why teens might be interested in participating in such a program. But which of their needs would be met with a library volunteer program? Here are a few that could apply to most teens in any community. Teens in other communities might have additional needs.

1. The need to fulfill their school requirements for community service hours.
2. The need to find college funding and/or college admittance.
3. The need to get work experience.
4. The need to make a difference in their community.
5. The need for social interactions and experiences.
6. The need to fill time in a constructive way.
7. The need to feel a sense of accomplishment and to be recognized as a person of value.
8. The need for a safe place to hang out.

According to a study examining the motivational needs of adolescent volunteers,[3] teens and adults differ in the factors that motivate them to volunteer. Previous studies have indicated that most adults, including college students, volunteer because of several reasons: a sense of social responsibility, a need for social contact, and the need for work experience. However, while adolescents were found to share the first two volunteer motives, the need for experience was not identified as an important factor for teens volunteering. What was the major difference between teens and adults? Teens cited the need for social approval, or affirmation, as their third major reason for volunteering. This response indicates that the developmental stages of adolescents affect their reasons for volunteering. Knowing and understanding these developmental stages is important in setting up a volunteer program for teens. They do have different needs from adults, so we must keep their physical, emotional, and social changes in mind when we develop the volunteer policies and procedures to serve their needs.

THE LIBRARY'S NEEDS

Does meeting teens' needs mean that a library's needs aren't met with a volunteer program? Of course they are. There are always tasks for teens to do that are extremely helpful to the staff. Honestly, volunteers can have a huge impact on library services. But having teens helping do these duties does not justify the time and effort of having the program. If we start with the needs of the teens, then we can minimize the frustration and aggravation that can result when the library's needs are not being met.

PLANNING

There are several steps in planning for a teen volunteer program. The best way to begin a program is to get some teens to participate in the process. Are there teens hanging out in the library? Invite them to a special meeting (with refreshments, of course) to find out what's important to them. What would motivate them to commit to volunteering? What rewards would interest them? What kinds of time commitments can they handle—two hours a week? Three? What kinds of tasks would they like to do? What ages should be included?

Then think about the staff who would be working with the teens. What are their needs? We need flexibility when working with teens, but we need rules, too. Ask the staff for their input. Do they have tasks the teens could do? Would they be willing to train the volunteers? Chat with them daily? Correct inappropriate behavior if necessary? Staff cooperation is essential to the success of the program. Involve them in planning as much as possible. Not only will they have good ideas to contribute, it will become their program, too. Successful programs depend on the participation of the entire library staff.

The third step, based on the information gathered from talking to the teens and the staff, is to determine the goals and objectives involved with the volunteer program. Goals can be defined in relation to the mission of the library, and each one describes a method of achieving one of the desired outcomes stated in this mission. The objectives are the ways in which the goal will be accomplished. For example, if a library wishes to reach the teens in its community, one goal could be to incorporate a teen web page onto the library website. One objective to fulfill this goal could be forming a teen web club, which would be responsible for designing, creating, and maintaining a teen website. Another objective could be to implement recommended reading for teens onto the site by recruiting teens to write reviews for publication of the books they have read. There could be a variety of objectives needed to accomplish the goal of adding a teen web page, depending on the library's resources and level of commitment to the project.

We have discussed the first steps in setting up a teen volunteer program. The volunteer program has been requested, justified, and approved. Teens and staff have been consulted and their advice incorporated into the planning. Rules have been decided; guidelines have been set. Goals have been determined and the ways to accomplish them have been listed. This planning was necessary in order to get the details needed to recruit, train, and support the volunteers for the volunteer program. I will discuss briefly the following steps in the process of setting up a teen volunteer program. Most of these steps will be described in more detail in later chapters.

JOB DESCRIPTIONS

The job description forms the basis for every aspect of a volunteer's experience in the library. It is imperative that each volunteer position has a job title and a job description. Each volunteer needs to know what is expected, and a job description not only explains the responsibilities of the position, it details the level of commitment required. Job descriptions can vary, but most include:

1. Job Title
2. Age or Grade Requirements
3. Supervisor's Name
4. Job Responsibilities
5. Time Commitment (weekly, monthly, temporary, ongoing)
6. Special Skills or Qualifications Needed (typing, lifting, driving, etc.)

Nothing more can happen with a volunteer program until the job description(s) is determined. Recruiting volunteers requires knowing what the volunteers will be doing. How can we decide what qualities to look for in potential applicants unless we know what skills and attributes are needed for the job? How do we train, supervise, evaluate, and recognize our volunteers unless we start with a description of what we expect from a teen doing the specified job? Most importantly, the job description demonstrates a well-designed and efficient program that plans for *all* aspects of a volunteer's experience in the library.

RECRUITMENT

Recruiting good volunteers takes creativity and energy. Unfortunately, the nature of working with teens results in a regular turnover of volunteers, and recruiting new teens to replace departing teens is a constant task. Librarians are always looking for good candidates even when they don't need applicants. The simplest way to recruit is to talk about volunteering wherever the teens are. And offer lots of rewards—happy volunteers don't quit as often. The following chapter will discuss the ways and means of locating and attracting appropriate candidate pools for a variety of volunteer positions.

13

HIRING

Each potential volunteer needs to be screened and interviewed before being considered for any position, and teenagers should undergo the same process as other volunteers. Often this is the first time that the applicant has ever been interviewed. Use the interview to find out why the teen wants to volunteer, what he or she hopes to learn from the experience, and what expectations will be placed upon the teen and the parent. Interviews are an important selection tool and should be taken seriously by everyone involved.

ORIENTATION AND TRAINING

Whether orientations take place one-on-one or in a group setting, time should be taken to show the volunteers where they will be working, what they will be doing, and most importantly, the rules they will be expected to follow. If contracts are to be used, explain them in detail before the volunteers sign them. Introduce them to as many staff members as possible. Tour the library and show them their work areas.

Training, however, should always be done individually or in very small groups. Young adults vary so much in their developmental stages that it's impossible to address each teen's need for guidance and instruction in a large group setting. Some young adults will grasp the rules of a summer reading program with one explanation; others will need it reinforced again and again.

STATISTICS

Count everything, whether you need it now or not. Count the number of volunteers, the number of hours they work, the number of books they shelve (if possible), the number of people they help—anything that might help justify the program if it is threatened. This information is also helpful to analyze the cost savings to the library if this work had been done by paid staff.

RECOGNITION

Most people work for money. Most teens would prefer to work for money. In fact, the reason most teens stop volunteering is because they are old enough to qualify for paying jobs. Even though most of us receive recognition for our work in the form of cash, this doesn't negate the other rewarding benefits we receive—or would like to receive for our efforts. As we all know, sometimes a verbal pat on the back from our supervisor means more than the paycheck we receive (well, almost). Volunteers also need those forms of recognition on a regular basis. Parties, candy, T-shirts, and gift certificates mean a lot, too.

EVALUATION

Evaluating the volunteer program is a required part of the process. There are several ways to do it. Talking to volunteers themselves is very effective, as is informally discussing the program with staff members. But evaluation isn't limited to the program itself. The volunteers should also be evaluated using a formulated set of criteria, both formally and informally. Regular evaluations can encourage good work while addressing any concerns that may have arisen about the volunteer's performance.

> Give teens meaningful work that makes them feel a real part of their library, praise and reward them whenever possible, and enjoy having them around. Teen volunteers allow other teens to see them in action at work in the library, and provide a model for teens to see that libraries are important.
>
> *Diane Tuccillo,*
> *Young Adult Supervisor,*
> *City of Mesa Library,*
> *Mesa, Arizona*

LEGAL ISSUES

Legal guidelines and ramifications regarding teens' volunteering in libraries can be overwhelming, if not downright scary. Some areas that *might* require legal advice are recruitment and discrimination, termination, safety training, and at-risk youth. This manual will not attempt to address the various legal aspects that can affect teen volunteer programs in libraries. Some libraries have volunteer coordinators who are extremely knowledgeable regarding volunteers and legal requirements and would be a good source for any questions. In addition, city attorneys can provide guidance if there are questions about legal issues regarding teen volunteers.

NOTES

1. "Normal Adolescent Development: Middle School and Early High School Years," American Academy of Child and Adolescent Psychiatry, 1997, www.aacap.org/publications/factsfam/develop.htm (27 July 2002).
2. "Normal Adolescent Development: Late High School Years and Beyond," American Academy of Child and Adolescent Psychiatry, 1997, www.aacap.org/publications/factsfam/develop2.htm (27 July 2002).
3. Connie K. Schondel and Kathryn E. Boehm, "Motivational Needs of Adolescent Volunteers," *Adolescence* 35, no. 138 (Summer 2000): 335–44.

3

Marketing, Recruiting, and Placement

Recruiting volunteers is a process that involves the extensive marketing, promoting, and publicizing of a library program to a targeted group of people, and it is directly tied to the type of person needed for the position. Since we want to reach teens, we have to know where to find them and how to attract them. This necessity leads to two questions: Where do teens spend their time? And secondly, how do we demonstrate that our volunteer program will benefit their lives?

Like any successful promotion, good marketing requires a strategy. Bonnie Mc-Cune recommends developing a four-part process based on marketing principles that emphasize the regulation of four items: product, place, price, and promotion. The product is the volunteer program, which has been developed according to the needs of the teens in the community and the needs of the library and its staff. Job descriptions list the types of duties to be performed, the special skills or abilities that might be needed, and the method of evaluation. The place is the library, or any other location where the volunteers will be working, which might appeal to potential volunteers. The third element is the price, which means not only the cost to the library of providing the program, but the worth of a volunteer's time against the benefits that are received. The fourth element is promotion, which can be done in three ways: personal contact with people who frequent the library; individual contact by means of flyers, posters, or phone campaigns; and mass media notices and articles that reach a wide audience.[1]

How do we translate these elements to attract teen volunteers? The product, our teen volunteer program, has been organized (see chapter 2) and just awaits candidates for consideration. However, the job description determines what kinds of applicants we will be seeking. Will they need special skills that will require recruitment of special individuals? What about the nature of their work? Will they work primarily with children? Seniors? Computers? Certain job requirements might change the focus of the promotional methods.

What about the place where the volunteers will be working? Is it in a busy corridor of the library with constant social contact? Or maybe the position is in the basement processing books—ideal for someone who likes to work alone. Are there comfortable chairs, a break room, a place to store personal belongings? Any options that can be offered as to location, time, tasks, or surroundings will open up more marketing possibilities and reach a wider group of teens.

VOLUNTEER PUBLICITY SLOGANS

Share, Grow, Participate

Do Good, Feel Good

Share Yourself

Energize Yourself

Take Time to Give Time

You Have It Within You

Helping Is Human

Together We Do It Better

You Are the Solution

Be a Hero

Make Friends, Learn Skills, Help Others

Join the Club

Make a Difference

We Need Your Help

Volunteers Matter

Work for Change

Get Involved

Donate Your Time

Lend a Hand

You're a Valuable Resource

Price has been discussed in chapter 1, but only in relation to the library in regards to having a volunteer program. Staff time is a hidden cost, but other investments are required. Budgets must reflect printing, orientations, training, supplies, and rewards. Everyone's time is valuable, including a teen's time. They are giving up something else in order to be at the library, so we want to make sure their contributions are valuable and worthwhile.

PROMOTION

Once the first three elements of product, place, and price have been determined, it's time to develop a promotional element to the marketing strategy. Previously we learned that young adults have several needs that volunteering may fulfill in their lives. The three most important are affirmation, social responsibility, and social contact. We need to utilize these aspects in our promotional flyers, notices, and conversations with teachers, parents, and the teens themselves. I'm not advocating using those exact words, but we can certainly appeal to potential volunteers by brainstorming possible phrases and terms that convey the same meaning. For example, if a group of seventh graders spends every afternoon socializing in the library, the librarian might approach them and ask if they ever thought of "getting credit" for volunteering at the library, where they could "really help the library get some work done" or "help others do better in reading." These phrases can be also be used in promotional flyers, news releases, posters, e-mail postings, or advertising. If we want to attract teens to volunteer work, then we should use the words and phrases that will speak to their needs. (For examples of this language, see the flyer from the City of Mesa Library at the end of this chapter. The descriptions in its "What," "When," and "Why" sections emphasize the rewards of helping the library. This threefold, double-sided brochure is created by printing its two pages back-to-back on one sheet, then folding into thirds.)

Each community has several places where teens hang out. The library provides many opportunities for personal invitations to volunteer. Other places to find possible applicants are local schools, scout troops, churches, sports programs, community centers, and local teen clubs. Visit them in person, if possible, to enthusiastically explain the volunteer program. Bring flyers to distribute, and send them anywhere else that teens might congregate. Contact teachers and ask to visit classrooms to promote library services and programs. Many local schools require their students to complete volunteer work before graduating. Although some libraries have problems accommodating the sheer numbers of students who want to volunteer at the library, such a requirement could still provide a steady source of applicants. Despite the communication and coordination problems, many libraries find that school community service programs provide many productive and satisfying volunteer experiences for both the library and the volunteer.

APPLICATION FORMS

Thoughtfully designed application forms can serve three purposes: they can publicize a volunteer program, function as a screening tool for potential volunteers, and provide information about various recruiting approaches. When designing an application, use attractive and eye-catching designs and pair them with catchy phrases that appeal to teens. We want to convey that volunteering at the library can be fun as well as work, so convey that sense of fun with lighthearted fonts, clip art, and wording. Some applications are folded so that the front panel is designed to attract attention to the volunteer program, then opens to reveal the specific information about the program and a simple form to be completed by the applicant. Other applications may utilize one side for a promotional flyer and the other side for the application form. (See two samples at the end of this chapter.)

When designing application forms, think carefully about the kind of information needed from the teen before and after the interview. What kinds of things would be good to know about the applicant in order to determine his or her potential as a volunteer? What questions would be better left for a personal conversation? Some supervisors might want to know about extracurricular activities in which the teen is involved; others might want to seek teens with special interests or skills. The specific position could lend itself to a question about related experience or knowledge. Notwithstanding the kinds of information being sought, the volunteer application should be short, simple, and precise, with few open-ended questions. Also, it is extremely helpful to include a brief description of the volunteer position, including age and time requirements, the type of work he or she may be doing, and any scheduling requirements.

Here are the elements of a Teen Volunteer Application Form:

1. Name, address, phone number, e-mail, and age of applicant
2. Name and phone number of parent
3. Social security number, if needed
4. School and grade
5. Days and times available
6. Space for the parent to sign the agreement for the teen to volunteer
7. Space for the teen to sign the agreement to follow library policies and procedures.

THE DARK SIDE

Some teens just don't want to volunteer. There is nothing wrong with this, but it seems there is always the parent who pushes their son or daughter into volunteer service when the teen would prefer not to participate.

One summer I started a reading program called "Ready Readers," in which teen volunteers read to young children in the library while their older siblings attended library programs. I did not conduct interviews but invited potential volunteers to an orientation (first mistake—interviews would have weeded out uninterested teens). One young man, about fifteen years old, attended the orientation but was not very engaged in my presentation nor interested in participating in any of the training exercises I had prepared. After about an hour of his sulking and sighing, I asked his mother why he came to the orientation, and she told me that she was aware of his reluctance but thought it would be "good for him" to volunteer. I let him sit there for another hour while the teens practiced selecting books and reading to each other (second mistake—he did not participate, and I should have let him leave). After the session, I asked the boy if he wanted to do this, and he said no. I told him he did not have to volunteer and I would explain things to his mother. The relief he felt was obvious. Better to be short a volunteer than have an unwilling and unhappy teen, who probably would have communicated his negative feelings to every child he read to during the summer.

Kellie Gillespie, Adult Services Librarian,
City of Mesa Library, Mesa, Arizona

Optional Application Questions:

1. What clubs or organizations do you belong to?
2. List any interests or activities you enjoy.
3. Why do you want to volunteer at the library?
4. Where did you learn about our volunteer program?
5. Do you have any experience with _____?

SCREENING

I wish there were a magic formula for screening applications in order to find good volunteers to interview. Employers have tried everything: handwriting analysis, aptitude tests, skills tests, supplemental applications—you name it. There are no generalizations, no rules, no fail-safe things to look for in an application that will ensure hiring a good volunteer. My only advice is to trust your gut. For some teens, this may be the first time they have ever applied for a job, volunteer or paid. It might be intimidating or even stressful for them. Maybe they put information in the wrong slots, crossed things out, left things blank—does it mean they will make a less-than-desirable volunteer? I have no idea. I do know, however, that some of the best teen volunteers have had the worst handwriting I have ever seen. While we may not want to hire an adult who can't seem to care enough to fill out an application properly, teens' applications should be viewed with a different set of criteria.

1. **They took the time to apply.** This means that unless their parents made them do it, they actually want to volunteer. Think about how hard it is for teens to get up on a Saturday morning, yet some have indeed made the effort to obtain the application, fill it out, and return it to the library. And they are willing to work on a Saturday morning! Okay, I realize this one is not foolproof. Maybe Mom picked up an application for Junior, stood over him at the kitchen table while he halfheartedly filled it out, and then drove to the library to turn it in. It does happen, but we can always screen out any reluctant volunteers in the interview.
2. **They are involved in outside activities.** I realize that a lot of teens are over-committed, but the same generalizations that are made for adults are usually true for teens: busy people are responsible people. They like to be busy and they keep their commitments. If the application lists other activities, that usually means that the teen is involved in the community and wants to make a difference in the lives of others.
3. **The reason they want to volunteer is because they are investing in their own fu-ture.** Maybe they are fulfilling a school requirement or looking ahead to college applications. It could also mean they want to gain experience for future employ-

Dear All-Knowing Teen Volunteer Guru,

My teen volunteer program can only accommodate five teens at any one time. This means that I can be really selective about who I hire, but it also means I have to turn away potential volunteers all the time. I feel like a heel rejecting all these great teens, but what other choice do I have?

Signed, Feeling Guilty

Dear Feeling Guilty,

First of all, guilt is a bad word in the young adult librarian world. Stop it, I say! Don't we have enough guilt about spending time with our own children without adding guilt about other people's children? Teen volunteer programs have enough issues without adding things like guilt to the mix.

It's actually a much better strategy to limit a teen volunteer program to a small number of volunteers. Smaller is better because you can spend quality time supervising, which will result in a better trained, more responsible, highly productive volunteer. It would be great to accommodate more teens, but you are wise to stick to your own limitations. It is better to be small and effective than large and chaotic. In addition, the volunteers that you've picked are aware that competition is fierce and they have an honored position in your volunteer program. They will work extra hard to keep their jobs.

Now, what to do about the teens not selected for a volunteer position? Call them and explain why they are not right for the job at this point in time. Tell them you will keep their application on file for a year—or whatever length of time you feel is appropriate. Encourage them to apply again in the future. Refer them to other agencies in your town that accept teen volunteers or the Volunteer Center, if you have one in your community. Some possible agencies for referral are museums, day care centers, parks and recreation centers, after-school programs, senior centers, animal shelters, zoos, school libraries, police departments, and hospitals.

Remember that rejection is a part of life. We can't shelter teens from feeling bad, but we can offer information and referral services to them so that they are aware of other opportunities. Let each applicant know that there are many volunteer positions available; soon they will find one right for them.

ment. Whatever their goals, they are demonstrating maturity, foresight, and responsibility by applying for a position that will help them succeed in life.

INTERVIEW PROCESS

Screening potential applicants continues with the interview. An interview can be difficult, painful, entertaining, confusing, informative, productive, or any combination

---

SAMPLE INTERVIEW QUESTIONS

1. Tell me about your favorite class at school.
2. Are you involved in any clubs or sports?
3. What do you like to do for fun?
4. What's your favorite kind of music? Or movie? (to get them talking and/or at ease)
5. Have you ever done volunteer work before? Tell me about it.
6. What do you hope to learn from volunteering at the library?
7. How will you get to the library for your shift?
8. Have you ever done the following activities? (work with small children, clerical work, etc.)
9. Do you like to figure out things for yourself or ask for help?
10. How would your friends describe you?

---

thereof. Again, it is often the teen's first interview experience, and he or she may have absolutely no idea what to say, how to act, where to sit, or even what to wear to this very important occasion. Once again, appearances do not indicate volunteer aptitude. Young adults might arrive dressed inappropriately, they might be too shy to meet the interviewer's eyes, or they might give monosyllabic answers to interview questions—but there is something about the teen that appeals to us. Maybe she lights up when we ask about reading to little kids. Maybe he created his own web page about his favorite music group and enthusiastically describes every detail of it to us. A few well-designed questions can draw a teenager out of shyness or nervousness and really show the potential that is waiting to be developed. Depending on the volunteer position to be filled, we can give most teens a chance to volunteer at very minimal risk. If teen volunteer programs are truly regarded as being for the teen, then in most cases, we really need to give the applicant an opportunity to volunteer, regardless of any negative first impressions we might receive at the interview.

These observations directly contradict interview protocol, don't they? Since most of the information available on interviewing is written for adults interviewing for paid positions, it is up to us, library staff working with teen volunteers, to invent new interviewing strategies to meet our library's mission and the needs of our teens. One library volunteer manual recommends trying to find volunteers that will fit the "departmental subculture and management style of the staff member in charge."[2] While this may be great advice for adults, it doesn't apply when interviewing teens. Teens don't fit anywhere, except with other teens, and often not even there. And how will they fit a management style if this is their first working experience? On the contrary, we should use the interview as a tool to get to know applicants, explain what we expect from a volunteer, find out their interests and skills, and determine if we can work together to meet everyone's needs.

There are several things that can be learned from an interview, even if we have different expectations from teens. The first is the level of parental commitment. It is strongly advised that one or both parents attend the interview along with their teenager. A parent who makes the time to bring a child to the interview is then more likely to help with transportation issues, and will probably remind the volunteer of the commitment when other activities compete for time. The interview is also a likely time to discover if Junior's mother is much more interested in Junior volunteering than Junior himself is. If Mom or Dad is doing most of the talking during the interview, it just might indicate that the teen has been coerced into filling out the application, has been forced to attend the interview, and most probably will not show up for any volunteer shifts of his own accord. Parental involvement is essential for successful teen volunteers, although too much involvement can send red flags to the interviewer.

Lastly, we can learn why the teen wants to volunteer at the library and where he or she heard about the volunteer program. As discussed previously, teens have a variety of reasons for volunteering, but it is interesting to learn why they chose the library out of all the opportunities that exist in the community. Their answers are often surprising. One teen said she wanted to volunteer at the library because of the swiveling chairs the volunteers used. She wanted to sit there and swivel back and forth on the chair while helping people. Okay, twelve-year-olds are still childish in many ways, but if this reason motivated her to try volunteering, it's as valid as any other. When we discover where the volunteer learned about the program, we can analyze this information to generate other promotional and publicity strategies—both for volunteering and for other young adult programs in the library.

In an interview, we can also learn what kinds of experience the teen has with different elements of the volunteer job, which helps with orientation and training. Teens who understand the library's classification system will need less training than volunteers who don't know how to locate books on the shelves. Their level of public service experience might also indicate what training options to provide and impact the kind of volunteer job for which they are most suited, if different positions are available.

NOTES

1. Bonnie McCune, "Marketing to Find Volunteers," *Colorado Libraries* 26 (Fall 2000): 40–41.
2. Preston Driggers and Eileen Duman, *Managing Library Volunteers: A Practical Toolkit* (Chicago: American Library Association, 2002), 71.

ADVICE FROM THE EXPERTS

We have a database for the public as a whole, the Berkeley Information Network, to which we refer teens (or help teens access and use) when we simply don't have the volunteer opportunities that suits their needs. One important thing I've learned in my travels among the libraries of California is that not enough information and referral seems to be happening when teens seek volunteer opportunities. We are in the information business and should be able to help them find a place to do volunteering even if it isn't at our library.

Francisca Goldsmith,
Teen Services Coordinator,
Berkeley Public Library,
Berkeley, California

HOW

Fill out the application attached.

WHO

Teens between the ages of 12-18 (eleven-year-olds can volunteer the summer following sixth grade).

WHAT

We depend on teen volunteers to help

- check out games
- cover books
- sort books
- set up for programs
- straighten shelves
- give directions

WHEN

Help us for two hours each week...after school, evenings or weekends during the school year and daytimes during the summer.

WHY

Volunteering helps you help others, and...

- teaches you job skills & values
- introduces you to other teens from other schools
- puts you in a great spot for doing your homework or reading
- makes you feel good
- it's fun!

WHERE

Youth Services Department
City of Mesa Main Library
64 E. 1st St.
(480) 644-2734

DROP BY

Mesa Public Library

We can use your help in our Young Adult Volunteer Program

Youth Services Department

CITY OF **MESA**
Great People, Quality Service!

Mesa Public Library
64 E. 1st Street
(480) 644-2734

City of Mesa Main Library
Young Adult Area
Volunteer Application

Date _____

Name _____

Address _____

City _____ Zip _____

Phone _____

Date of Birth _____

School _____

Grade _____

Special hobbies or interests:

_____

_____

Other activities or clubs:

_____

_____

What are your reasons for volunteering?

_____

_____

_____

Volunteering is like having a job. We count on you to be here at a certain time. Volunteers are asked to work at least two hours a week.
What times can you work as a volunteer?

Days _____

Times _____

IN EMERGENCY, CONTACT:

Name _____

Home Phone _____

Business Phone _____

Name of Parent or Guardian

_____

Address _____

Phone _____

Signature of Parent or Guardian consenting to applicant's working as a volunteer:

_____

I hereby apply for work as a volunteer in the Young Adult Area of the Mesa Public Library. *

_____
Applicant's Signature

_____
Date

* You will be contacted when an opening occurs.

mesalibrary.org
City of Mesa Library on the Web

10/01

Tucson-Pima Public Library

Teen Volunteer Application Form

Name:_____ Home Phone:_____

Address:_____City_____Zip_____

Are you age 14 or older? Y N   Emergency Contact:_____

School:_____Grade:____   Phone:_____

Give two personal references we could call and talk to about your abilities (teachers, counselors, or other adults not related to you).

Name:_____Position:_____Phone:_____

Name:_____Position_____Phone:_____

1. Have you volunteered before? Yes_____ No_____ If yes, where?_____

2. Please list the skills and experience that you possess which can be utilized in your volunteer service with the Library.

3. Why do you think you want to volunteer at the library?

4. Please list any interests, hobbies, clubs, activities, or special skills:

5. Are you required to fulfill a specific number of volunteer hours?_____ If yes, how many?_____

At which branch do you want to volunteer?_____

Days you can volunteer: (circle) Sun Mon Tue Wed Thu Fri Sat
Times you can volunteer: From_____ am/pm to _____ am/pm
First day you can volunteer:_____Last day:_____

List any days you will not be able to volunteer for special reasons:_____

_____

Signature:_____ Date:_____
(I attest that all information above is accurate and true to the best of my knowledge)

Parent Signature:_____ Date:_____
(Required if teen is under age 18)

TUCSON-PIMA PUBLIC LIBRARY
TEEN VOLUNTEER PROGRAM

- ## WHAT WILL I BE DOING AS A TEEN VOLUNTEER?
  Examples of teen volunteer activities:
  - During the summer months, assist librarians during busy times by handing out and explaining summer reading program materials to children or teens.
  - Alphabetize children's books by author and shelve them.
  - Straighten up books on shelves and straighten up furnishings in children's room.
  - Help with children's programs:
    - Help set up meeting room before programs.
    - Help clean up and organize meeting room after program.
    - Take attendance at the door and count children.
  - Gather and arrange books for children's book displays.
  - Tape and jacket books.
  - Prepare craft materials.

- ## WHAT WILL I GET OUT OF IT?
  - An opportunity to learn and practice a variety of job-related skills.
  - Satisfaction from knowing that you are helping to promote reading and literacy in your community.
  - Something different and interesting to do.
  - An opportunity to meet new people.
  - A pleasant, air-conditioned working environment during the long, hot summer.
  - Volunteer experience, a welcome addition to college, scholarship, and job applications.

- ## WHO IS ELIGIBLE FOR VOLUNTEERING?
  - Teens who want to (not because their parents are making them do it)!
  - Teens who are self-motivated and reliable.
  - Teens who are 14 years old or older.

- ## HOW DO I GET STARTED?
  - Fill out the attached application and turn it in to the Information Desk at any participating library branch. The Volunteer Coordinator will contact you.

If you have any questions about the program or application, feel free to call:

NAME: **BRANCH:**   **PHONE#:**

Library
Address
Tucson, AZ 857

4

Orientation and Training

Orientation and training differ in several ways. Orientation is a general introduction to the library, the department, the staff, the rules and policies, and an overview of the volunteer job itself. Training, on the other hand, is a very specific demonstration of the tasks that the volunteer will be doing. Orientations can be done formally or informally, in a group or individually. Training should be done informally and either individually or in a very small group.

ORIENTATION

Everyone is nervous when starting a new job, and since this is a new experience for most teens, they will be even more apprehensive about attending an orientation. Plan the event to be informal, relaxed, and fun. Parents should also attend the orientation, so carefully select a day and time that is convenient for them, too. Volunteer orientations can take a variety of formats—intense one-hour sessions or a half-day informational and "get-acquainted" workshop, for example—but most will include the following elements:

- **Welcome.** Express to the teens how much they are appreciated and how excited the staff is to work with them. Thank the parents for their support and encouragement. If the library director or department supervisor is available, their welcoming words will validate the library's commitment to the volunteers and the program.
- **Introductions.** Introduce any staff who will be working with the teens. If possible, briefly describe the staff's responsibilities and how they relate to the volunteer's tasks. Each staff member could also say a few words of welcome and offer their help to the volunteers if they have any questions.
- **Job Duties.** Give an overview of the volunteer tasks that they might be doing. General instructions are okay, but save any training or demonstrations for later.
- **Attendance.** Explain the expectations regarding the volunteers' attendance. Go over the procedures if they are absent due to illness or vacations. Be very specific about whom to contact if they can't make their shift, and provide any information they will need if substituting or trading among volunteers is allowed.
- **Conduct.** Be very clear about expectations regarding conduct in the library. Are the volunteers allowed to eat or drink while on duty? What about talking or visiting with friends? If they have public contact, give an overview of appropriate versus inappropriate ways to talk to library customers. Most libraries are committed

ADVICE FROM THE EXPERTS

Here at the Berkeley Public Library, we try to make the experience of volunteering also one of learning about the variety of jobs—and their attendant requirements—in the library. We train everyone to understand some basic tenets of public libraries: confidentiality of information as well as intellectual freedom. Teens seem to be very conservative when faced with the prospect of young kids hearing "bad" words or learning about social problems. We also tell them what to do if someone makes them feel uncomfortable—that they should seek a (paid) supervisor's intervention rather than trying to deal or failing to deal with it themselves.

Francisca Goldsmith, Teen Services Coordinator, Berkeley Public Library, Berkeley, California

THE DARK SIDE

Those of us in the library world know that libraries can be weirdo magnets. A strange man approached one of our teen volunteers as she was hanging out in the library after her shift. He offered to take her to a fast food restaurant. She declined and thought no more about it until she was outside the library on her way to a convenience store. He pulled up next to her and tried to persuade her to get in the car. When she refused, he kept following her and scared her pretty badly. Not knowing what else to do, she came back to the library and we called the police.

Equip volunteers with the knowledge they need to keep themselves safe. They should be observant, aware, and cautious at all times, whether they are on duty or just spending time in the library. Encourage them to report any suspicious behavior to staff at once.

ADVICE FROM THE EXPERTS

It's a good idea to plan for and provide a bin or box filled with items the teens might need while on volunteer duty. Some helpful things to include in the box are feminine hygiene products (different kinds), change for the bus or phone, nonperishable food and drinks, extra name tags, a first-aid kit, sunscreen (if they are outside while on duty), and any other items they often need and forget to bring from home.

Kellie Gillespie,
Adult Services Librarian,
City of Mesa Library,
Mesa, Arizona

to providing a high level of customer service to their patrons, and volunteers are an important aspect of providing this quality service

- **Reference Questions.** Explain the difference between directional and reference questions. Some libraries don't want volunteers answering reference questions, even if it's helping to locate a book. Clearly define what kinds of questions volunteers can answer for customers and which questions they should refer to a staff member.
- **Safety Concerns.** We don't want to alarm teens or their parents, but safety can be an issue in our libraries. Talk about the potential for dangerous situations that might exist in any public building. Inform them of evacuation procedures. Also, tell them that they should immediately tell a staff member if anyone—library patron or library staff member—bothers them or makes them feel uncomfortable in any way. Reassure them that we are committed to a safe and enjoyable volunteer experience for everyone.
- **Dress.** What is allowed and what isn't? Give specific examples as far as clothing, shoes, jewelry, and hair, if necessary.
- **Policies and Procedures.** Even if this information is included in handouts distributed at the orientation, it's a good idea to emphasize important library policies. These may include library cards, lending periods, Internet rules, confidentiality, library fines, name badges, parking, telephone use, breaks, and any other rules they need to know.
- **Library Tour.** Take the group around the library. Show them their work space(s) and time sheets, if needed. Show them locations for supplies, staff breaks, vending machines, and any storage areas to which they might need access. Introduce them to the public services staff as they are encountered. Bring them into staff work areas and show them staff entrances to use before the library opens.
- **Volunteer Guidelines.** Some supervisors find it helpful to develop a volunteer handbook to distribute to teen volunteers. It can be anything handed out to volunteers for future reference—a few pages stapled together or a small bound booklet. Some libraries create a folded brochure with a minimum of information to hand out to teens. Others include the library's history, general library information, policies and procedures for volunteers, and a library map. Any handouts should reinforce the information discussed at the orientation and include contact information, absence procedures, dress guidelines, appropriate volunteer behavior, and any other rules that might need repeating. (See two examples of such handouts at the end of this chapter. From the Caviglia-Arivaca Branch Library is a booklet for printing on two sides of a single page with a single vertical centerfold. From the Tucson-Pima Public Library is a standard single page.)

TRAINING

Effective training is not easy. In most cases, it has to be individualized to fit the learner's needs, which means it takes a lot of time, patience, and demonstration. It also takes a great deal of trial and error before deciding on the training method that works best for the volunteer and the type of work that he or she will be doing. In her book, *Training Student Library Staff*, Lesley S. J. Farmer recommends that trainers consider a variety of learning styles, make the training useful and meaningful, use hands-on training activities, accommodate mixed abilities, let teens share their experiences, and make it enjoyable. Most volunteer training will be task-specific with an immediate practical use. Because of individual learning styles, some volunteers will need more direction and repetition than others will, especially younger teens who have fewer skills and experience. In addition, other factors can interfere with effective learning, such as a negative reaction to criticism, bad experiences in the past, a lack of interest in learning the task, or insufficient instruction.

Farmer's book is helpful in that it approaches training as part of a total education process. Since training is a form of teaching, it is appropriate to consider carefully all aspects of the tasks that need to be learned in relation to the person learning them. According to Farmer, there are several steps involved in creating effective training sessions. The following list is modified to include other library settings.

1. **Determine the training objectives.**
   - Who needs the training?
   - What are the desired results?
   - What will the training enable the volunteers to do?
2. **Design the training.**
   - What do the volunteers already know?
   - What different learning styles can be addressed?
   - How much time is needed to do the training?
   - Who will conduct the training?
   - What is the format to be used: demonstration? computer tutorial? videotape?
   - What handouts are needed to support the material?
   - How will the training be evaluated? How will you know if they have learned the material?

ICEBREAKERS OR PARTY GAMES

- Set up chairs in a double circle facing each other and have each person sit opposite his or her partner. Give them a topic to discuss, such as school or music groups. Play music (as in musical chairs) while they get up and walk around the chairs until the music stops. They find new places opposite someone else. Give them a new topic to discuss. Repeat this routine several times until everyone gets to know several people.

- Tape a book or cartoon character's name to each person's back. They have to guess whose name is on their own back by asking questions of others.

- Sit the volunteers in a circle. The leader chooses a subject that distinguishes people from each other. For example, food, colors, playing an instrument, etc. The leader calls out, "Stand up if you like blueberries," and some people will stand up and some will stay seated. The people standing up then have to find another seat and another subject is called out. The leaders can be switched so that different people have a chance to lead the group.

- Cut up old posters or banners into puzzle pieces and let teams race to put them together.

- Lie the kids on the floor in some kind of pattern. Start with one end and have that person say, "Ha." The next person has to say, "Ha Ha," then the next person says, "Ha Ha Ha," and so on until someone starts laughing.

- This game is called "Two Truths and a Lie," and it is borrowed from the Sylvia Beech Inn in Portland, Oregon. Each person makes one false and two true statements about themselves and the group has to guess which one is a lie.

Public Librarians, YA-YAAC Listserv, May 11, 2001

3. **Conduct the training.**
   - Define the task and desired results.
   - Demonstrate the task for the volunteers.
   - Let volunteers share reactions.
   - Explain the process.
   - Check for understanding.
   - Have the volunteers practice applying the process.
4. **Evaluate the training.**
   - Content: level of difficulty, usefulness, and relevance
   - Delivery: presentation style, pacing, simplicity, time frame
   - Resources: handouts, audiovisual aids
   - Student performance: task completed to satisfaction

A variety of training methods can be used to teach teen volunteers effectively. Since people learn in different ways, it is advisable to incorporate several methods into a training session. Practicing the tasks is essential to the process of learning them; provide adequate practice time for every volunteer before expecting the task to be completed. The training methods used most often to train teen volunteers are: presentations, demonstrations, case studies, and peer-training. Presentations are the most common way to provide information to students, but should be supplemented with visual aids, discussion, and hands-on activities. Demonstrations are used to model correct techniques. They should be simple and direct, with follow-up questions and practice. Examining case studies provides volunteers with opportunities to apply the knowledge they have learned to specific examples to solve real-life problems. Other methods to reinforce the training can include completion checklists, visual instructions, tutorials, and videotapes. These reinforcement techniques can help a volunteer who has learned the tasks but needs a little memory boost to complete them.[1]

POSSIBLE VOLUNTEER TASKS
BOOKS

- Book sales–organize, price, staff, clean up
- Cover paperbacks with plastic laminate
- Repair books
- Process books
- Search for missing items on shelves
- Clean books
- Attach genre stickers

Clerical

- Word processing
- Photocopying
- Stuff envelopes
- Inventory supplies
- Collate and staple handouts
- Create and maintain spreadsheets

Collection Support

- Check booklists against catalog
- Search the web for new sites
- Read reviews and recommend items for collection
- Create booklists of recommended books
- Shelf reading
- Check usage statistics
- Repair magazines

Facility Maintenance

- Dust bookshelves
- Straighten magazines and newspapers
- Vacuum
- Clean tables and chairs

Programming

- Create props
- Make puzzles
- Make name tags for story times
- Take photographs
- Pass out programs
- Help with craft projects
- Staff summer reading desk
- Read aloud to younger children
- Make reminder phone calls to registrants
- Assemble and disassemble tables and chairs
- Pass out evaluations
- Crowd control
- Registration for programs
- Count participants
- Check catalogs for teen prizes
- Rewrite stories into other formats—flannelboard stories, puppet show scripts, finger puppet stories, fingerplays, and songs
- Decorate for parties

PUBLIC SERVICE

- Schedule public computer terminals
- Maintain computers and workstations
- Fill scrap paper and pencils
- Clean monitors and keyboards
- Teach public how to use computer applications, e-mail, or navigate the Internet
- Help public find materials
- Create and maintain web pages for teens

PUBLICITY

- Bulletin board displays
- Book displays
- Distribute flyers
- Visit schools with librarians to promote teen programs
- Design and produce ads, flyers, or posters for programs

NOTES

1. Lesley S. J. Farmer, *Training Student Library Staff* (Worthington, Ohio: Linworth Publishing, 1997), 37–39.

Caviglia-Arivaca Branch Library

You Deserve A Break Today!

If you need to use the restroom or get a quick drink from the water fountain, go right ahead. If you will be gone for more than 5 minutes, please let someone know before you go.

It's also okay to use the telephone, just keep your calls brief.

Teen Volunteer

Booklet

Caviglia-Arivaca Branch Library
17050 W. Arivaca Road
Arivaca, AZ 85601
398-2764

Library Hours

Day	Hours
Monday	Closed
Tuesday	11am-8pm
Wednesday	11am-8pm
Thursday	10pm-6pm
Friday	11am-5pm
Saturday	9am-5pm
Sunday	Closed

Welcome!!!

Thank you for volunteering your time at the library.

This booklet is for you to keep! It contains all the tidbits and doo dads of information you need in order to be a teen volunteer!

Make sure that you have filled out and turned in your Teen Volunteer Application so that the library has it on file.

What to Wear

The library is not very picky about what volunteers wear while they work. However, if you follow these guidelines, you'll be safe:

- The more skin covered, the less likely that wardrobe will become an "issue."
  (It hovers around 70 degrees in the library)
- It is not necessary to wear personal views.
- Chances are, if it's inappropriate at school, it's also inappropriate while volunteering at the library.
- The best way to protect those toes is to keep 'em covered.
- Neat is better than messy.
- Sweatpants are not preferred.
- Jeans, long shorts, and sneakers are okay.

While at Work...

From time to time you will likely see a friend or two while you're working. Of course, you can say, "HI!" Please keep your visiting to a minimum, however.

???Questions???

It is very likely that in the course of your volunteer work, customers will ask you questions. If they ask location questions such as, "Where is the restroom?" go ahead and give them the answer. Otherwise, refer them to the Information Desk where one of the librarians will help them.

Where Do You Go?

If you will be volunteering before the library is open, please enter through the Staff Entrance on the North side of the building. If you will be volunteering during library hours, please use the public entrance. Please report to a member of the Reference Staff to learn the duties of the day.

Uh-Oh! Who Do You Call?

If you need to schedule your hours, report that you will not be at work, or inquire about any other concerns, please call **791-4393**. If you need to reach the library before it is open, call the *Emergency Only* number: **791-2647**. Leave a message for the Young Adult Librarian

Tucson-Pima Public Library
Teen Volunteer Orientation & Training

- **WELCOME!**

  The Library welcomes you as a volunteer member of the library staff. Thank you for your interest in becoming a teen volunteer. Your time, energy, and talent enable our library to continue providing a high level of service. We hope your association with the library meets your needs as well as ours.

- **POLICIES AND PROCEDURES**

  Volunteers are considered members of the library staff and have the following rights and responsibilities:

- **Attendance**

  Schedules are planned to give the library coverage needed to provide adequate and efficient library service. Volunteers are depended upon to work the hours they are scheduled. Promptness in coming to work is expected. Please notify the Volunteer Coordinator in the event of absence or tardiness. Please try to give adequate notice of planned absence so that schedules may be rearranged.

- **Volunteer Name Badges**

  Volunteer name badges are to be worn by all volunteers on duty. Volunteer name badges help library customers distinguish between volunteers and paid staff and also serve to promote the volunteer program.

- **Dress**

  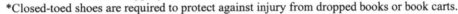

  Volunteers are asked to dress appropriately for working public service. Specific guidelines:
      *Closed-toed shoes are required to protect against injury from dropped books or book carts.
      *Jeans are acceptable, but ragged, frayed or cut-off jeans with holes in them are inappropriate on the job.
      *Please refrain from wearing sweatpants.
      *T-shirts with messages or promotional graphics relating to drugs, alcohol, or sex are prohibited.

- **Conduct**

  Friendly, efficient service is expected at all times. Since the public sees you as a staff member, you represent the library and its commitment to excellent service.

  Try to be pleasant and courteous to everyone using the library, regardless of their demeanor. If you are not absolutely certain how to answer a customer's question, refer her/him to the staff member at the Information Desk. Questions relating to the location of books and other library materials, and reference questions, should always be referred to staff at the Information Desk.

  Visits or personal telephone calls are not appropriate in a place of work. If you must contact someone, wait until you are not on duty. Emergencies (sudden illness, for example) or the need to inform your family of an unexpected change in scheduling, are considered library business, and you are welcome to use the library telephones for these purposes.

  Food and drink are not permitted in the library except in the staff areas. Smoking is not allowed anywhere in the library.

   THANK YOU!!!

5 Recognition and Retention

Everyone needs validation. Even if we get paid money for working, we all appreciate a pat on the back every once in a while. It's even better if our accomplishments are broadcast to lots of people, so that everyone knows how wonderful we are and what a great job we do. Teens are no different. Of course, they would like money, but most libraries don't have the means to pay teens for their time and effort. So we have to think of creative and fun ways to reward all our volunteers for their hard work. Often praise can be incorporated into a formal or informal evaluation of a volunteer, which should be done on a regular basis, but teen volunteers should be thanked by other means as well. Happy volunteers usually stick around for a while, so retention and recognition are related and interdependent activities.

Retention efforts are difficult with teenage volunteers. They are, naturally, a busy and changing group, with many factors that might affect their volunteer status at any one time. The big factors happen at age sixteen, when two life-changing events occur: They can get a driver's license and they can get a job. But many other factors affect their volunteer status: parents' time and level of commitment; access to transportation; homework, school, and church activities; home responsibilities; and a variety of other reasons. This situation does not mean that we have failed to retain them as volunteers; it just means that they have other demands on their time—some more appealing than volunteering, some over which they have no control. If we want to keep our volunteers past the driving and working stages of their lives, we must concentrate our efforts on rewarding them with tangible and intangible gifts and awards that are directly related to the reasons they volunteer in the first place: their need for social contact, social responsibility, and social approval.

Any effort to recognize volunteers should start with a plan. A formal recognition policy will include several components: recognition criteria, special volunteer awards, publicity, a schedule or timetable, and budget. Having a formal recognition policy is the best way to ensure fairness and consistency with all volunteers while recognizing that different groups of volunteers will appreciate different kinds of rewards. For example, a group of teens who were recruited for a short-term project such as a summer reading program might receive just

> **INEXPENSIVE RECOGNITION GIFTS THAT TEENS WILL LIKE**
> - Candy—any kind, any amount
> - Fast food gift certificates
> - Bookmarks
> - Video store gift certificates
> - T-shirts or hats with library logo
> - Sports bottles or mugs filled with candy
> - Pencils and pens
> - Notepads/notebooks
> - Magnets
> - Keychains
> - Theater gift certificates
> - Posters
> - Paperbacks

NO-COST WAYS TO RECOGNIZE VOLUNTEERS

- Say thank you
- Tell them they did a great job
- Suggest they join you for a soda or a snack
- Ask them their opinions
- Give them more responsibility
- Greet them when they come into the library
- Show interest in their personal lives
- Smile when you see them
- Take them along when shopping for library purchases
- Brag about them in their presence
- Let them select something for the library
- Tell them a joke and let them tell you one
- Jot small thank-you notes and attach them to their sign-in sheets
- Say something positive about their personal appearance
- Give them a special privilege
- Ask them about the last book they read or TV show they watched
- Put funny stickers on their time sheet
- Let them have first pick at discarded posters, books, etc.

one special reward when their term of employment is completed. Volunteers who work year-round, however, might receive a series of rewards throughout the year based on the number of hours they work, their helpfulness to staff or the public, each year of service, completion of a special project, an innovative idea, or just because they volunteer their time.

The criteria used for recognition will vary according to the type of event or reward used, but it should be consistent for all volunteers. There are three basic ways to recognize volunteers: regular reinforcement done by the supervisor to support the volunteer's efforts, special gifts or rewards given individually to acknowledge volunteer service, or events that collectively recognize groups of volunteers. Teens' motivational needs can be met using any of these methods, but the most effective is the positive reinforcement given on a regular and frequent basis by the volunteer's immediate supervisor. Such reinforcement is effective because it is a constant reminder of the volunteer's importance to the supervisor and to the organization. It is so easy to do—simply acknowledge the volunteer's efforts each and every time he or she comes in to work.

These methods of recognition can be done in two ways: informally or formally. Formal recognition is usually done via dinners or receptions where the volunteers are honored collectively with individual awards for specific achievements. Generally speaking, teens prefer anything informal, especially if food is involved. Some libraries have formal affairs or programs with cloth napkins, waiters serving fancy food, and motivational speakers. In my experience, most teens don't appreciate this kind of recognition. If able to choose, teens would prefer the money be spent on something more fun for them, like a pizza party or an ice cream social. Using the same set of criteria as adults, informal events can include special awards just as formal events do—without the podium and microphone. There are so many more options available for informal parties, from silly awards presented to each volunteer (such as "best joke-teller" or "most likely to become a librarian"), to games played inside or out, to activities such as bowling or swimming that the event can be structured around.

One of the best volunteer parties we had was at a local swimming pool that had picnic facilities. The library paid for the teens' admission to the pool and lots of soda; a local pizza delivery chain donated the food. The volunteers swam and ate pizza and then the volunteer supervisors each spoke briefly about the volunteers' contribution to the library and how much they were appreciated by the library and the community. The three of us then presented a skit that we had prepared to illustrate how much we needed their help. We portrayed a helpless patron who needed lots of guidance, a har-

RECOGNITION PARTY THEME IDEAS FOR TEENS

Olympics

Possible slogans: Volunteers Are Winners; Volunteers Are Our Gold; Volunteers Are Gold Medalists

Fill water bottles with candy ("volunteers are special" bottles if desired). Greet each teen by hanging a gold medal around his or her neck. Decorate the room/area with red, white, and blue bunting and streamers. Design a variety of "first place" awards and have various staff members present them with a few words of appreciation. The awards can be certificates, specially ordered plaques, or even funny items that accompany the award given. One special touch would be to create a video highlighting teen volunteers at work with the Olympic theme music in the background. Another idea is to create a display using this theme with pictures of teens and other Olympic-related items.

Hats

Possible slogans: Hats Off to Our Volunteers, Hats Off to You

Staff can wear silly and funny hats. Hang hats on the wall as decorations. Make hats—either newspaper hats or wide brimmed hats with tape around the crown and the brims rolled up. Have an assortment of ribbon, buttons, sequins, balloons, and anything else that could be used as decorations. Use upside-down hats filled with flowers for centerpieces. Design the room so that the volunteers have to get up and move around to decorate their hats, thereby meeting other volunteers.

Valentines Day Thank You

Possible slogans: We Love Our Volunteers; Volunteers Give from the Heart

Use lots of red and white bunting, streamers, flowers, and balloons. Put big bowls of candy hearts around the room and on the tables. Take instant pictures of each volunteer, along with some group shots, and place on heart frames. If desired, let the volunteers decorate their own frames and post on a library display board to recognize the volunteers. Serve heart cookies, cupcakes, chocolate dipped strawberries, and other valentine-related items. Give each volunteer a special valentine's card with a personal note expressing your appreciation for his or her service to the library.

ADVICE FROM THE EXPERTS

I send a letter (easily personalized on the computer) to each member of the Teen Volunteer Corps each month, thanking him or her for donations of time the previous month (if any) and telling about upcoming needs for volunteers. If a teen is interested, he or she calls or e-mails us to sign up for that activity. *That's* when the firm commitment comes in. We tell people we're counting on them to be where they said they would be and when. And we are! None of the volunteer opportunities are busy work.
Hope Baugh, Young Adult Services Librarian, Carmel Clay Public Library, Carmel, Indiana

ried librarian too busy to assist him, and Super Volunteer, who saved the day with lots of patience and advice. The teenagers seemed to appreciate our silliness—there was much laughter and teasing about our costumes and acting ability—but the message got across and at minimal cost. The adults had as much fun as the volunteers and everyone went home filled with pizza and good feelings.

There are so many ways to recognize teen volunteers that I hes-
itate to make a list because I'm sure that many resourceful librarians have discovered their own successful rewards. In addition to
parties or other events, recognition can include awards and gifts.
Awards can be certificates, plaques, pins, buttons, or any other
item that must be earned by a predetermined set of criteria. Many
items can be special-ordered and inscribed with the achievement
and/or the volunteer's name. In most cases, such items require a
substantial budget investment and can also create some competition among volunteers. Gifts, on the other hand, are handed out
to every volunteer for a specific reason or as a general appreciation
for their work. Holidays, birthdays, and events such as National
Library Week or National Volunteer Week can all be occasions for
little gifts to thank a volunteer.

However volunteers are recognized and rewarded, there are several "rules" that should be followed.

1. Do it. Recognize teens for their volunteer efforts or they won't
   volunteer. If we don't recognize their efforts, volunteers feel as
   if they don't matter and what they do doesn't matter. Then they
   will quit and tell their friends not to volunteer either.

2. Do it frequently. Praise has a short life; it feels good today but
   we forget it tomorrow. It's human nature to want positive reinforcement on a regular basis.

3. Use different methods. This advice goes with #2. Giving praise
   frequently means that it should vary or else volunteers end up
   hearing the same thing over and over.

4. Give it honestly. Recognizing mediocre work minimizes the
   recognition. There's something to praise for every effort.

5. Recognize the person, not just the work. Volunteers want to
   hear how they make the difference, not the program or the
   results.

6. Make it fit the task. Reward small tasks with a small acknowledgment, big accomplishments with a major celebration.

7. Give it consistently. Similar rewards for similar duties.

8. Do it in a timely manner. Teens need immediate recognition for
   a good job. Don't wait until the next general party or event.

9. Do it on an individual basis. Get to know the teens and what is
   important to each one so that the rewards mean something to
   each recipient.

10. Reinforce good behavior. If negative behavior receives attention, then those volunteers who are behaving appropriately and doing their job might feel neglected. Recognize positive conduct and see it more often.

One thing is certain. Teens are like everyone else—they want to feel appreciated and to know that their volunteering makes a difference. Make sure to communicate that appreciation every time they are recognized for their efforts.

ADVICE FROM THE EXPERTS

We used our fine money to buy snack-size candy bars on sale after holidays like Halloween or Valentine's Day and used them to fill the Candy Bucket. We never had a problem getting students to work in the Learning Resource Center because after their shift each student was rewarded by getting to choose a piece of candy out of the bucket. The reward thing was huge! We got kids to help us with anything—moving furniture, setting up chairs—for a little candy bar. Our only restriction was they could have one piece and they couldn't eat it in the Learning Resource Center.

Every year we asked for and received money from a special school fund that we used to give every student volunteer a five-dollar certificate to a fast food hamburger chain or the local ice cream store. We also used our fine money to buy them candy canes or something at Christmas. For really special volunteers, we sometimes would buy a paperback.

The school also recognized students at "Honor Breakfasts" during the year. Parents were invited before school started and were served doughnuts and juice. Usually it was to honor students with good grades or those who had participated in a seasonal sport. Finally they agreed to honor students for other accomplishments. During the last honor assembly of the year, we sent in the list of students who had worked for us during the year. They all got invited to the Honor Breakfast! It was a big thing for a lot of our volunteers who would otherwise never have fulfilled the criteria to be invited to an Honor Breakfast.

Chris Carlson, VOYA *Advisory Board*
St. Charles, Illinois

SOURCES FOR VOLUNTEER GIFTS

4-Imprint
877-446-7746
www.4imprint.com

ALA Graphics
866-746-7252
www.alastore.ala.org

Amsterdam
800-833-6231
www.amsterdamprinting.com

Best Impressions
800-635-2378
www.bestimpressions.com

Harrison Promotions
800-929-2271
www.harrisonpromotions.com

JanWay
800-877-5242
www.janway.com

Promo Unlimited
800-748-3326
www.promounlimited.com

Upstart (division of Highsmith)
800-558-2110
www.highsmith.com

Voluncheer
408-792-3456
www.voluncheer.com

6 Supervising Volunteers

It takes a special person to supervise teen volunteers effectively. Sure, anyone can hire a few teens, show them what to do, and get them started. Of course, when they quit after two weeks, this kind of manager gets to do it all over again with a new group of volunteers. It takes skill, experience, organization, time management, nurturing, coordination, teamwork, and patience to supervise teenagers effectively so that they stay in the program for any length of time. Actually, the best teen volunteer supervisors have several different roles: cheerleader, fund-raiser, disciplinarian, activities director, taskmaster, and guardian. The hardest part? Knowing the right part to play with each teen at any given time.

For the most part, teens can benefit from general supervision techniques that are detailed in management manuals. Some common tips that can be applied to supervising teens are:

1. Hire effectively to ensure that the worker fits into the organization. Hiring the right match can avoid problems later on.
2. Care about the employee or volunteer. Demand quality work, then recognize and reward the achievement.
3. Be clear and concise about assignments, then give the worker the authority to accomplish the job.
4. Design effective job descriptions. New duties should be assigned according to the skills and abilities of the employee or volunteer.
5. Allow adequate training time and follow-up to make sure that the volunteer knows what to do and how to do it.
6. Be flexible and open to alternative solutions. By taking more time to consider various possibilities, supervisors become leaders, not bosses.
7. Communicate openly with others. Sharing information with employees means that they are trusted so that productivity increases and morale is high.

EVALUATION

Performance evaluations can be a valuable tool to the volunteer manager. Not only can evaluations serve as an opportunity to offer feedback to volunteers about their work, but they can also provide feedback to the supervisor about the volunteer program. They also can isolate any problems, either in the program itself or with the volunteer, that the supervisor might not know about. There are many methods of appraising the volunteer's performance in the library. Whatever form is chosen, teens will benefit from a series of informal and formal meetings to talk about how things are going with them. Such meetings are not a time for criticism or punitive measures; the purpose is to help the volunteer examine his or her own performance according to a set of criteria that reflect the current mission of the volunteer program. There is a practical benefit to formal evaluations—they provide a record of the volunteer's performance when the student needs a recommendation letter for work or school. This record really helps when someone calls five years after volunteering and the supervisor has no recollection of the volunteer, let alone his or her work performance.

Most volunteers want to do a good job. Discussing their performance provides them with positive feedback and gives value and respect to their work. It should not replace the daily coaching and problem-solving that is involved with supervising. In fact, informal work appraisal should be a regular part of supervising the volunteer, so that any small performance problems can be corrected as they occur. Informal discussions can also isolate any problems the volunteer might be having and provide a quick means of solving them. Formal evaluations, on the other hand, should be part of an evaluation policy that includes a regularly scheduled meeting between the volunteer and the supervisor in order to discuss job performance and satisfaction. The first such meeting should be scheduled about a month after the volunteer begins and annually after that.

Any performance appraisal must begin with the job description. The job description outlines the goals, objectives, and tasks involved with the job. Any measure of a volunteer's performance of that job should reflect these expectations. If a form is to be used, make it as simple as possible, with sections on quality of work, attitude, relationships with others, and a place to record goals and/or growth opportunities. Discuss the job description and whether the volunteer needs more responsibility. Most importantly, listen to what teens have to say about you and the volunteer program. Ask questions about the training they received, whether they like their job, and how things could be improved. In the past, I have given volunteers a form to evaluate the program. They fill it out ahead of the scheduled meeting time and bring it with them so we can discuss their responses candidly. The teens have made some great suggestions and offered valuable insights about recognition, staff attitudes, job duties, and my supervision style and techniques. Some of it was hard to hear, but helpful and necessary in order to improve the volunteer program and my own supervisory skills.

EVALUATION FORMS

Performance appraisals for teens should be very simple. As I've mentioned before, this is the first working experience for many teenagers, and getting called into the supervisor's office can be scary. When my supervisor tells me she needs to talk to me in her office as soon as possible, I get a little nervous myself now and then, especially when she says, "Close the door," with a serious look on her face. Design the evaluation form to cover several aspects of the job, depending on the volunteer job description. Three

> Dear All-Knowing Teen Volunteer Guru,
>
> Obviously you don't work in the real world. I have my hands full with 30 volunteers, ages 12 to 17. They need to be trained how to cover books with plastic laminate, a process that takes at least 30 minutes for each volunteer, plus be shown how to do the summer reading program for the little kids. Let's not even go into my regular librarian duties of working 20 hours a week on the reference desk and weeding my entire fiction collection by August 30. There are only 24 hours in each day—how on earth am I supposed to do evaluations TOO?
>
> Signed,
>
> Longing for Fall
>
> Dear Longing,
>
> The All-Knowing Teen Volunteer Guru empathizes with your situation. You are not alone—we all have felt the stress of having too much work to do. But trust me, having a written record of each volunteer will save you time in the long run. Not only can the evaluation address potential issues before they become problems (and take up even more of your time), but it promotes volunteer retention, which means fewer teens to interview, train, and evaluate! It also saves time when the teen calls for a letter of recommendation in five years and you rack your brain trying to remember whether he did a good job or not.
>
> If you have a lot of volunteers to evaluate all at once, such as summer volunteers, an alternative solution could be to distribute individual written evaluations, but discuss the summer program in a group setting. Or you might decide to save evaluations for the teens who successfully complete the summer session. Or maybe someone else in the library can take up some of your other duties for a period of time during evaluations. The benefits far outweigh the time commitment—and the feedback process helps you become a better volunteer supervisor, which makes the program more worthwhile for everyone involved.

good overall categories that encompass most volunteers' work experience are quality of work, attitude, and relationships with others. Decide on a system to measure the volunteer's performance in these areas, such as grades, a number system, or some other easy code. Leave room for personal comments, which can include explanations, more details, or anything not covered in the given categories. Don't forget the volunteer's evaluation of the program, which offers the opportunity to rate the program from his or her perspective, such as supervision, training, job and tasks, and how the program could be improved. I recommend giving each teen the completed evaluation and the blank volunteer's evaluation of the program several days ahead, so that he or she can have time to reflect before the scheduled meeting. (See examples of both the supervisor's and the volunteer's evaluation forms at the end of this chapter.)

THE DARK SIDE

The staff in the children's room complained long and hard about a teen volunteer who seemed to think she was a librarian. She even wore little eyeglasses on a chain and her hair in a bun. She was a good worker who did whatever task was asked of her, was always on time, conducted herself in a professional manner, and was pleasant to library patrons. The problem? She frequently corrected staff members when they were in the middle of a reference transaction—usually in front of the patron. The staff people being corrected often told the teen that they could handle the question, thank you very much, but she didn't get it. She was an equal-opportunity enforcer, even correcting me, her supervisor, on occasion. After several gentle reminders that the library staff could handle the reference questions, I scheduled a meeting with her and explained in frank terms that she was annoying the library staff and she needed to stop correcting them. She agreed to stop and did—for a while. When the behavior began again, I detailed the problem in writing on her annual evaluation, and we talked about it during another meeting. Her behavior improved permanently after that discussion; seeing the problem in writing seemed to make the difference.

Kellie Gillespie, Adult Services Librarian,
City of Mesa Library, Mesa, Arizona

PROBLEM BEHAVIOR

We want all of our volunteers to succeed. The best way to insure success is to set up an environment with sufficient training and communication that enables volunteers to do their jobs with a minimum of problems. We need to be clear with our expectations and enforce them consistently. We also need to equip the volunteers with the skills and materials to do their jobs properly, which requires sufficient time to train them properly. Training must include clear instructions for doing specific tasks, repetition, and following up to make sure the volunteer has mastered the skills needed to fulfill the assigned jobs. Communication is central to the success of the volunteer, and it must be mutually honest, open, and trusting. It is the supervisor's responsibility to make sure the volunteer understands what is expected of him or her, but it is the responsibility of the volunteer to communicate any problems he or she is experiencing. Since many teens feel uncomfortable doing that, we must spend lots of time with our volunteers to create an environment in which they can talk easily about issues they are experiencing.

Most problem behaviors are easily remedied by simply talking to the volunteer privately. Be brief and specific describing the undesirable behavior and what is expected of volunteers. Explain that because library staff and patrons require a high level of service from volunteers, this behavior is disappointing. If necessary, explain what the consequences for repeating the behavior are. The supervisor's demeanor should be professional; don't smile while discussing such a serious subject. Put the problem in perspective, however, especially if it's a first-time offense. If the volunteer has done good work in the past, point that out and express confidence that he or she will continue to show good judgment in the future. Above all, assure the teen that everybody can learn from these things, and as long as the behavior is not repeated, it will be forgotten and life will go on as usual in the library.

Lesley S. J. Farmer suggests that volunteer managers look closely at the type of problem behavior in order to see if there are possible reasons. She lists several representative scenarios in her book, *Training Student Library Staff.* I have modified her list for use in other library settings.

1. **Sloppy Work.** Causes could include insufficient training, incomprehension of task, not enough resources, or not enough time. In addition, the volunteer could have physical or learning disabilities that interfere or distract, or there could be a contradictory attitude.

2. **Low Productivity.** Causes could include insufficient training, incomprehension of task, not enough resources, distraction, contradictory attitude, or perfectionism.
3. **Inconsistency.** Causes could include distraction, conflicting priorities, or stress.
4. **Disrespect.** Causes could include lack of self-esteem, unawareness of own actions, insufficient training, or a contradictory attitude.

Although distractions can have many sources, some are under the volunteer's control and some are not. If it seems that a behavioral issue is caused by distraction, the volunteer and the supervisor might be able to talk about possible solutions to the problem.

Behavior problems can result from a teen's immaturity and/or inability to cope with feelings. According to Farmer, teens might be experiencing certain needs that are reflected in associated behaviors that are often undesirable. The following is a list of misguided behavior goals and ways the volunteer manager can immediately handle them.

1. **Attention.** This goal is characterized by behaviors such as clowning around or being forgetful or negligent. The appropriate response is to ignore the behavior, redirect it, or give choices to the volunteer.
2. **Power.** This goal is characterized by behaviors such as aggression, defiance, disobedience, hostility, stubbornness, and resistance. The appropriate response is to withdraw from the power struggle, cool off, and approach the volunteer later with several ways to solve the problem.
3. **Revenge.** This goal is characterized by behaviors such as rudeness, violence, destructiveness, and retaliation. The appropriate response is to withdraw from the conflict, cool off, and suggest alternative solutions later.
4. **Feelings of Inadequacy.** Such feelings are characterized by passive behaviors. The volunteer might want to quit, avoid making an effort, or escape through drugs. The appropriate response is to be patient, avoid showing pity, and celebrate small successes.
5. **Superiority, Excitement, Peer Acceptance.** These goals are often characterized by behaviors such as risky conduct, avoidance of routine, ingratiation, or insults. The appropriate response is to explain safety policies and redirect to positive actions.

Problem solving involves several steps: understanding the problem, brainstorming alternatives, evaluating the alternatives, choosing a solution, and evaluating the solution. It is best to meet with the volunteer to undergo this process together so that each has input and can find a solution that meets everyone's needs. However, if the problem is a result of a library policy or procedure that needs revising, other library staff might need to be consulted.[1]

THE DARK SIDE

Freddy was causing lots of problems as a young adult volunteer. He wandered away from the service desk during his shift, telling us he was going to the restroom and returning forty-five minutes later. He threw library cards at youth patrons instead of handing them back. He wanted to pick and choose the tasks he did instead of doing what needed to be done. After discussing these problems several times, the volunteer coordinator and I drew up a work agreement that clearly spelled out the unacceptable behavior and necessary improvements he needed to make in order to continue as a library volunteer. We had a meeting with Freddy and his mother, had them both read and sign the agreement, and notified him that he was on probation for six months.

His parents were very supportive of our efforts and tried to make Freddy aware of the consequences of his actions. Unfortunately, he did not improve his behavior and still left the service desk for long periods of time while on duty. We thought perhaps he was too young to volunteer and could be considered again when he was more mature. The volunteer coordinator remembers him crying in her office for more than twenty minutes when she terminated his service. She gently ushered him out, but later found him huddled in the library stairwell, still crying.

This incident happened about five years ago. Freddy came to visit us last year. He told us that he later was diagnosed with Attention-Deficit Disorder and that getting fired was the best thing that had ever happened to him. It was good to see that he still loved the library and did not hold his termination against us.

Kellie Gillespie, Adult Services Librarian,
City of Mesa Library, Mesa, Arizona

TERMINATION

Firing a volunteer is always regrettable but sometimes necessary. It is never the desirable outcome, especially in teen volunteer programs. It is always the last resort, always heart-wrenching, and *always* an admission of failure on the part of the volunteer management. However, before any termination, certain policies should be in place. If they are, it's very possible that no teen volunteer or volunteer supervisor will ever have to experience termination.

The first step is to decide whether the volunteer program allows teen volunteers to be terminated. If volunteers in other library programs can be terminated, then the same criteria should be applied to teens. There are several valid arguments for developing a volunteer policy regarding termination. It is important to have the same level of high customer service to library patrons held accountable for all employees, whether paid or not. Having a different set of standards for volunteers cheapens the value of their contribution. Their work has the same level of relevance and importance that is given to paid staff; having the same high expectations gives value to volunteer service.

Having a termination policy does not mean that it is a desirable action. Several alternatives can be utilized very successfully before it is necessary to resort to such a painful action. Steve McCurley recommends trying any of the following approaches to remedy problem behavior. I have modified his list for use with teen volunteers.

- **Re-Supervise.** Some teens periodically test the limits set by authority figures. Go over the policies and procedures of the library and the teen volunteer program. If necessary, have teens sign a contract stating their agreement to follow the rules and the consequences if any rule is violated.

- **Re-Assign.** If the teen is having problems with a particular task, or if he or she is not getting along with another volunteer or staff member, it might be possible to place the teen in another setting if alternatives are available, such as a branch or department. Otherwise, changing shifts might help the situation.

- **Re-Train.** Sometimes in our hurry to get teens through orientation and training and actually on the service desk, we might miss someone who needs an extra helping of instruction. Maybe this volunteer needs a different method of instruction, such as one-on-one demonstrations, or to be paired with an experienced volunteer who can take the time to go over each aspect of the job.

- **Re-Vitalize.** If a teen has been around for several years, he or she might just need a break from doing the same tasks over and over. Extra responsibilities could provide a change, such as mentoring younger volunteers, training, recruiting, or even moving to another department to take on new challenges.

- **Refer.** It's possible that the teen isn't working out at the library because of issues such as scheduling, transportation, or the nature of the job. Referring a volunteer to another agency can be an option. Better yet, talk to staff at a branch or another library about sharing volunteers who feel bored or need a break. They can spend a few months at each facility and get a little perspective and variety to add to their experience.[2]

It might happen that a supervisor tries all these methods to correct a teen's behavior, work performance, and/or attitude, and nothing seems to improve matters. In this situation, it's important to have the termination policy and procedures in hand so that the process cannot be questioned if it resurfaces in the future—such as when the volunteer's parent calls you for an explanation. A part of the policy should include documenting offenses and a graduated series of consequences for repeated violations of the volunteer program rules. For example, the first offense can be documented in the volunteer's evaluation. The second offense can result in the volunteer being put on probation, with the understanding that a third offense will mean termination. This policy doesn't mean that a supervisor will give teens only two chances to get their act together, but it does give recourse to the supervisor when he or she finally loses hope in a volunteer's potential for improvement.

Probation is a great tool to motivate a teen to improve behavior and/or work performance. The documentation and consequences should be presented to the teen and parent in a scheduled meeting. Both should sign an agreement or contract stating the unacceptable behavior, the consequences of continuing that behavior, and the time limit of the probationary period. It's an excellent opportunity to discuss the behavior itself: why it is unacceptable, why the teen is doing it, and what alternatives are available to the teen. Sometimes other needs become apparent in this kind of meeting, such as more training or a different schedule. The parent's involvement is absolutely essential to the probation process. A parent might know of a learning disability or behavior problem that is affecting the teen's performance. In some cases, this meeting will reveal that the parent is not supportive of the teen's involvement in the volunteer program, which means the supervisor and the teen must develop a different strategy to deal with the problem.

Firing a volunteer usually means a conflicting set of emotions for the volunteer supervisor. The feelings are mixed because it is sad to lose a volunteer in these circumstances, but it is a relief that the problem has been resolved. If and when it becomes necessary to fire a volunteer, here are a few tips to help with the experience:

ADVICE FROM THE EXPERTS

Motivation is the number one factor in a volunteer's success. I think when looking for teens one should always be cautious if a parent is calling to say the teen wants to volunteer.

I also think the statistics are true—if a teen has a negative volunteer experience, he or she will probably never volunteer again. It is very important that a volunteer's time is never wasted and that work is well planned and prepared in advance.

I embrace the philosophy that libraries should expect to give more to the teen volunteers than the reverse. We can build skills and confidence in young people, we can engage their spirits, we can turn them on to reading, and we can give them job skills and public service skills. Some teens give way more than we could ever imagine!

Engaging young adults in public libraries is one of the most intelligent things we can do. They are our future patrons and taxpayers and will carry it on to their children. We also owe it to our community to keep kids off the streets by giving them good things to do, and mostly, by believing in them.

Janice Gennevois, Volunteer Coordinator,
City of Mesa Library, Mesa, Arizona

Meet with the volunteer privately. Don't expose him or her to the curious stares of others. Make sure that the teen has an exit that preserves his or her dignity and privacy.

Be quick, direct, unemotional, and absolute. Use wording that clearly states the situation and the outcome. Make sure the teen knows this decision is unfortunate but final. Do not allow any argument.

Do not counsel or offer further guidance. It is too late for further help, which should have been offered earlier if it was an option.

Allow the teen to express emotions. A terminated volunteer might feel sad, angry, or frustrated. As long as behavior is not threatening or violent, allow some time to vent in a quiet and respectful way. If behavior becomes argumentative or abusive, then terminate the meeting.

Document the situation and inform staff. Send the volunteer a follow-up letter with the action detailed in writing. Update the teen's file for future reference.

NOTES

1. Lesley S. J. Farmer, *Training Student Library Staff* (Worthington, Ohio: Linworth Publishing, 1997), 32–34.
2. Steve McCurley, "How to Fire a Volunteer and Live to Tell About It," *CASA Resources* 1993, www.casanet.org/program-management/volunteer-manage/fire.htm (12 Aug. 2002).

Volunteer's Evaluation of the Program

Volunteer _____

Job Assignments _____

Volunteer Manager _____

Please respond to the following questions. Your input will help make the Volunteer Program more responsive to the needs of the Library.

1. Supervision

   A. Were your duties explained to you before you started volunteering? _____

   B. Did your job include duties not described until you started volunteering? _____

   C. When you needed information, was your manager available? _____ Yes _____ No _____ NA

   D. Were you included in your department's meetings, training, etc.? _____ Yes _____ No

   Do you want to be scheduled for meetings? _____

2. Training

   A. What type of training have you received in your position? _____

   B. Were you satisfied with the training you received? _____ Yes _____ No _____ NA

   C. Have you been able to use the training material? _____ Yes _____ No _____ NA

   D. Do you have any suggestions for improving training for this position? _____

   E. Is there any other type of training you would like to receive that would assist you in completing your volunteer duties? _____

3. Job Content

   A. Do you find your job enjoyable? _____ Yes _____ No If no, what would you like to do? _____

   _____

   B. Does the staff seem appreciative of your work? _____ Yes _____ No

   C. Do you find your co-workers to be supportive? _____ Yes _____ No

   D. In your work with other volunteers, do you find them supportive? _____ Yes _____ No _____ NA

   Please explain _____

4. Do you have any other comments or suggestions for improvements?

   Supervision _____

   Recognition of Volunteers _____

   Recognition of Staff _____

   Job Orientation _____

   Patron Services _____

   The Overall Volunteer Program _____

_____ _____
Volunteer's Signature   Date

City of Mesa Public Library
Volunteer's Annual Progress Review

Volunteer Evaluated _____

Evaluated By _____ Position _____

Job Assignment(s) _____

1. Evaluate the volunteer's performance (**Exceeds Standard, Meets Standard, Needs Improvement, Not Applicable**) in the following areas.

   A. Quality of work

      1. Accuracy in fulfilling duties _____

      2. Completion of assigned tasks _____

      3. Follows directions _____

      4. Job knowledge _____

      5. Ability to identify and solve problems on the job _____

      Comments _____

   B. Attitude toward job

      1. Flexibility _____

      2. Dependability _____

      3. Promptness (if applicable) _____

      4. Initiative _____

      Comments _____

   C. Relationships with others

      1. Communication with staff _____

      2. Rapport with other volunteers (if applicable) _____

      3. Patron rapport _____

   D. Volunteer job description - Please review, update if necessary, and attach changes to current job description.

2. Did the volunteer or volunteer group demonstrate other significant qualities such as leadership skills?

   Explain: _____

   _____

   Assume additional responsibilities _____ yes _____ no If yes, please explain _____

   _____

3. Attach any recommendations, comments, or complaints reflecting the volunteer's work.

_____   _____
Volunteer Manager's Signature   Date

_____   _____
Volunteer's Signature   Date

7 Volunteer Program Variations

Although the basic information presented in this manual is applicable to most general library volunteer programs that are geared to teenagers, there are always different circumstances that require special consideration. The following programs have been included here because they are different. They may have different requirements regarding supervision, attendance, management philosophy, and/or agency cooperation, and therefore require more documentation and inter-agency cooperation. These variations can mean more work for the volunteer manager. School volunteer programs, on the other hand, have a distinctive environment that changes the flavor of the program, even though the volunteer procedures regarding hiring, training, retention, and supervising are certainly applicable and appropriate for use in a school setting.

COURT-ORDERED VOLUNTEERS

Court-ordered community service volunteers undergo an alternative means of punishment as minor offenders of the judicial system. Many times these offenders are young adults. The decision to accept court-ordered teens as volunteers should be given a lot of consideration. Some libraries do and some don't. In most cases, the decision not to accept them is due to one or all of the following factors: It requires more documentation and accountability from the volunteer's supervisor; working with volunteers who have a criminal history can be intimidating to staff and patrons; and it can create liability issues that library administration prefers to avoid.

If court-ordered teens are involved in a library volunteer program, it is vital to establish a policy on the types of offenses that will and won't be accepted. Most offenses committed by teens are minor and might be related to drugs or alcohol, traffic violations, or shoplifting. The majority of libraries that do accept court-ordered volunteers will not consider anyone convicted of violent crimes. The volunteer manager has the right to know the nature of the crime committed by the teen before committing to hire him or her for community service in the library. The supervisor must make sure that the volunteer is treated the same as others in the program and that the teen's privacy is maintained while working in the program.

Supervising court-ordered volunteers can be difficult. Obviously, the teen did not choose to volunteer and might show a lack of enthusiasm for the work to be done. It might be necessary to remind the teen that there are other jobs available to complete their hours of service—such as picking up trash along the highway or cleaning toilets in

THE DARK SIDE

I've had kids who are a little lazy, leave for the bathroom and don't come back for fifteen or twenty minutes, make all kinds of excuses for being late or not showing up, are painfully slow in completing tasks, try to hang out with their friends while volunteering—but one teen has done all of those things and more. She was awarded one hundred hours of community service when she was out after curfew in a car full of guys, and then allegedly gave the judge some attitude. She only completed twenty-four hours with me and then decided not to show up anymore. She has since found out that her alternative is jail, so the judge is giving her one more chance and we'll see how it goes. This girl (age fifteen) lied to me more that I thought anyone was ever capable of—she started out with a fake doctor appointment, then relatives started dying, then she told me that she had after-school detention two days a week. She also told the school that she couldn't have detention on those two days because of her commitments at the library, but she was really out with her friends! (The principal and I eventually caught up to each other and figured it out.) Needless to say, I'm a little wary about taking her back—we'll see! The first time she messes up, I'm supposed to contact the judge and she'll be on her way to juvenile detention. She's currently on house arrest; apparently she's been in a lot of trouble since I saw her last.

Teen Volunteer #2 is another court-ordered teen (thirteen years old), who missed four appointments for our interview and then didn't speak to me at all during the interview. When I scheduled him for his first day (I'm a glutton for punishment, obviously), he didn't show, we rescheduled, and he didn't show again. When I sent in his paperwork documenting this situation, he went to his probation officer and said he wanted another chance. He probably got his second chance somewhere not quite as nice as the library.

Kimberly Paone, Young Adult Librarian
Elizabeth Public Library, Elizabeth, New Jersey

the local park. There can be other problems associated with using these kinds of volunteers. They need close supervision, they often miss their assigned working times, and they might think that it is the library's responsibility to meet *their* needs instead of the other way around. If they are accepted into the program, however, it is important that they be given the same benefits and responsibilities as the other volunteers, as well as be required to follow the same rules and expectations.

There are benefits to accepting court-ordered teen volunteers. Recruitment is easy: There is an endless supply of teens looking for an "easy" work assignment. Of course, they soon find out that working at the library requires their attention, their diligence, and their concentration. Indeed, some might be wishing they were working outside cutting grass instead of shelving picture books in the children's room on the first day of the summer reading program. Another benefit comes with the knowledge that the volunteer *needs* to finish her hours—or else! "Or else" means that they have to explain things to their parents, the judge, or both. "Or else" might also mean that they will spend time in a correctional facility if they don't finish their time at the library. Sometimes this leverage helps if attitude or attendance problems arise. The best benefit, however, is knowing that this volunteer job might have an impact on a person and change his or her life forever.

SCHOOL VOLUNTEER PROGRAMS

Because school media centers are located within schools, they have to be defined within the school culture to be effective. Lesley S. J. Farmer details several components that define a school's culture in her book, *Training Student Library Staff*:

- **Student Profile:** Socioeconomic background, geographic areas, transportation, student values, popular students and their groups, postsecondary options.
- **Community Profile:** Parents' careers and values, parents' involvement, neighborhood characteristics, school's relationships to community.
- **Faculty Profile:** Socioeconomic backgrounds, educational backgrounds, teaching and classroom management styles, faculty/administration relationship, social encounters.
- **Academic Profile:** School's mission, curriculum, yearly/daily schedules, counseling for students, staff development opportunities.
- **Governance:** How decisions are made, spoken and unspoken rules, who enforces the rules, administration's role, school/district relationship.[1]

These profiles must be considered when setting up a school volunteer program. What kinds of tasks will volunteers be doing? Is transportation available in the community? Will the faculty and staff provide encouragement and support to a teen volunteer program? What kinds of students will be recruited? When can they volunteer during the school day? Because a school media center has a limited pool of volunteers—students—the program must be geared to the teens who attend that school. Determining the school's culture and working within that culture will ensure an effective and successful school volunteer program.

SERVICE LEARNING

Service learning is a vague term that means different things to different people, depending on the institution and its understanding of the concept. In most cases, it describes a volunteer requirement that schools place on students. Students have a certain amount of time to volunteer at an outside agency for a predetermined number of hours in order to graduate. In its truest form, however, service learning is more of a learning experience than a volunteer experience. The goals are for the student to receive instructional and developmental opportunities in order to further his or her education and career goals. To accomplish these goals, the volunteer and supervisor work together to create achievable objectives that will be accomplished during the time the student volunteers. Mark Cooper offers the following characteristics of service-learning programs:

1. Community service serves as the vehicle for the achievement of specific academic goals and objectives.
2. It provides structured time for students to reflect on their service and learning experiences through a mix of writing, reading, speaking, listening, and creating in small and large groups and individual work.
3. It fosters the development of those "intangibles"—empathy, personal values, beliefs, awareness, self-esteem, self-confidence, social responsibility, and helps to foster a sense of caring for others.
4. It is based on a reciprocal relationship in which the service reinforces and strengthens the learning, and the learning reinforces and strengthens the service.
5. Credit is awarded for learning, college-level learning, not for a requisite number of service hours.[2]

ADVICE FROM THE EXPERTS

The majority of our student volunteers worked during the study hall periods. During our combination lunch/study hall/band periods, students were at lunch for half the time and attended band practice or study hall for the other half. Usually, the better behaved and more serious students were in band, and the study hall teachers sent the "problem" students to the media center. When I took over as Learning Resource Center director, I began to limit the number of students from each study hall to five per day. In later years I revised that policy; a student could only come twice a week. I felt that it was only fair to share the discipline problems with the study hall teachers.

We discovered that a good way to engage these students was to put them to work. Since we insisted that students from study hall read or do homework while in the library, we did a big business in magazines, which we displayed behind the circulation desk. The primary job of the student volunteers was to take care of the magazine checkout during the study hall periods. They made sure the kids signed them out and returned them at the end of the period, putting them in the right place on the shelf. We also had them stamp date due slips, take out all those nasty subscription cards that fall out of the magazines, cut things that had been laminated, put pencils and paper by the computers, and do other little things we could find for them.

I don't want to give the impression that all our volunteers were either average kids or ones with learning disabilities. We had several girls who were honor students and just wanted to help out. I love working with kids (the one thing I do miss now that I am retired), and it was just fun to get them involved in helping out in the library and find out what made them tick. I found that as long as you treat them like "real people" and give them a reward, kids are more than willing to help out.

Chris Carlson, VOYA Advisory Board,
St. Charles, Illinois

This system is obviously very different from what most public libraries have experienced with students trying to fulfill their service-learning obligation. I believe, in many cases, "service learning" is becoming synonymous with "community service." They have very different objectives, however. Service learning is a learning-based program that centers around the needs of students who work in an organization to achieve specific goals that are designed to enrich their instructional experience. Community service is a service-based program that centers on the organization. It is hoped that by requiring students to volunteer at community agencies, they will gain an appreciation of the community's needs and their value as a contributing member of that community.

Because service learning is academic and requires coordination with school faculty, I don't believe most public libraries participate in this type of program. Rather, libraries participate in helping students with community-service requirements for students in local junior high and high schools. In most cases, volunteer managers simply accommodate these students within their existing teen volunteer programs by utilizing the same policies and procedures that are used for the other teen volunteers. The only difference, usually, is a timesheet or letter that must be signed by the supervisor and returned to the school.

There has been some debate about schools requiring students to complete community-service time in order to graduate. Several state legislatures have passed laws that allow school districts to require a certain number of volunteer hours, which can range from 10 to 120. Supporters of this requirement argue that the volunteer requirement is beneficial for students. It builds confidence and self-esteem, enables future voters to become involved in their communities, and exposes them to a wide variety of people, situations, and experiences. Some schools require students to reflect on their volunteer experience by writing a paper or turning in a journal. The wide variety of volunteer opportunities ensures that students can find something of interest, whether serving food at a homeless shelter, painting murals at a daycare center, helping build a house, or walking dogs for an animal rescue organization. Sometimes teens need encouragement to volunteer; community-service requirements provide that encouragement.

Opponents of the community-service requirement for school graduation argue that it is unfair and unwise to force anyone to volunteer. How can it be volunteering if it's mandatory? Doesn't the very nature of volunteerism require a willing and giving heart free of resentment and stress? This is a valid argument; volunteerism should be an open and honest donation of time, talent, and energy freely given. Forcing someone to volunteer takes away this gift and makes it an obligation. Furthermore, some say, today's teens have plenty of homework, extracurricular activities, and after-school jobs to keep them busy. They don't need another thing in their busy lives. Despite these objections, it is a fact of life that community service is here to stay for many communities. Those of us who work with teen volunteer programs in libraries need to be prepared to handle the added demand for placement.

There can be several problems with community-service teens. One recurring issue that many libraries face is the procrastinating teen who has waited until the last possible day/week/month to contact the library about fulfilling their volunteering obligation before the deadline. Experienced managers have learned to say no—often and emphatically. Secondly, community-service volunteers sometimes want special treatment—they don't want to undergo training requirements, for example, since they only have a few hours to volunteer. However, community-service volunteers need to be treated exactly the same as any other volunteer—application, interview, orientation, training, etc. And finally, some teens with this requirement are not exactly enthusiastic about working. If they don't exhibit the appropriate attitude or motivations that a supervisor is seeking, then they can be referred elsewhere to complete their service. Many teens seem to feel that they are entitled to do their service anywhere they want. It is our job to remind them that is a privilege to work at the library, and this privilege must be earned.

Many libraries across the country are taking advantage of community-service requirements for teens by developing specific volunteer opportunities to accommodate this increased need. This could be an excellent time to expand a summer volunteer program to the school year. It could also provide an occasion to establish relationships with schools and teachers in the community, which could lead to other programming and publicity cooperation. I realize that the community-service requirement can be frustrating and time-consuming for young adult librarians to accommodate, but I hope that we can focus on the positive aspects of encouraging teens to volunteer, especially at public libraries. Anything that brings teens to the library is a good thing; we need all the help we can get.

NOTES

1. Lesley S. J. Farmer, *Training Student Library Staff* (Worthington, Ohio: Linworth Publishing, 1997), 9–10.
2. Mark Cooper, "Big Dummy's Guide to Service-Learning," Florida International University, www.fiu.edu/~time4chg/Library/bigdummy.html (12 Aug. 2002).

How Do They Do It?
Interviews with Teen Volunteer Managers

Jeanette Cohn, Library Director

Rockaway Township Free Public Library, Rockaway, New Jersey
www.gti.net/rocktwp

Rockaway Township is located in northern New Jersey, about thirty-five miles west of New York City, with about 23,000 residents. There are five elementary schools and one middle school located in the city and two regional high schools just outside the city limits. The library employs twenty-eight individuals at two branches; ten are full-time. The library receives its budget from the township, state aid, and donations, fines, photocopier money, and fax money. The library board of trustees is the governing body and consists of seven members appointed by the mayor. They are responsible for library policies, planning, and the budget.

There are two young adult volunteer programs, one during the summer and one during the school year. Jeanette Cohn coordinates all the summer programs including the teen volunteer program. During the summer of 2002, they had sixty-two teens volunteering two hours per week each. The teens are scheduled for a particular time. They monitor the summer reading club program by checking off the reading logs of reading club participants and giving out prizes each week to readers. They mark off how many books the child has read onto a list of participants. The teens also cut out name tags for an entire year's worth of story times. The library has eighteen to twenty story times each week for four sessions (winter, spring, summer, fall). The teens also assist the storyteller with crafts and other special activities. The library director, the children's librarian, and the reference librarian work with the teen volunteers. The children's librarian is responsible for training and scheduling the volunteers. During the school year, teens may volunteer after school to assist in the afterschool Chapter One Club. And the library can always use volunteers to help take care of the garden.

What is your background? How did you get to this point in your career?

JC: I am the library director. I was going to become a teacher; however, I decided in my senior year in college to seek another career. I was tired of spending my life in school. A college guidance counselor recommended librarianship. I worked as a library page in the local library for a short time. I then decided to go to library school, which was Queens College in New York. In September 1967, I became a library Head Start worker at the Queens Borough Public Library, where I planned and conducted story times in an underprivileged community in South Jamaica, Queens. In January 1968, I became a librarian trainee at the Broadway Branch of the Queens Borough Public Library.

I received a masters degree in library science in January 1969 and was promoted to assistant branch head of the Middle Village Library. A little while later I became the branch head of that library until 1972. In 1979, after my children were four and seven years old, I became a storyteller at the Rockaway Township Library. In September 1980, I was hired as a Principal Children's Librarian. In 1986 I became an assistant director, and in 1988 I became the director.

How long have you been working with teens? What are your other duties? What other teen programs/services do you offer?

JC: I have been working with teens since 1990. My other duties include management and supervision of the entire library. We do not offer other teen programs due to the wide variety of programs offered by the schools and by our town's recreation program.

What do you do during your volunteer orientations?

JC: During the one-hour teen volunteer orientation, the children's librarian explains the summer reading club program for that summer and details of the teen assignments. She tells them about checking in each week and calling if they cannot come in for their shift.

What is your favorite thing about working with teen volunteers? What is your least favorite thing?

JC: I love the enthusiasm of the teens and the kind way they are with the children. The least favorite part is having to repeat instructions to each of them, since they only work two hours a shift. Instructions change during the summer as the program progresses. It is difficult to keep the teens abreast of these changes.

What do you expect from the teens who volunteer? Do they meet your expectations? Do you evaluate them? How?

JC: The teens are expected to arrive on time, call if they cannot make it, and be friendly and accommodating to the public. At the end of the summer each volunteer receives a teen volunteer letter of appreciation. They are not evaluated.

Which teen volunteer do you remember and why?

JC: I remember the volunteers that I personally work with on Mondays, Wednesday evenings, and Friday mornings. They were wonderful this summer. One boy in particular was very mature, always willing to stay longer than his shift, and very polite.

What methods do you use to train your teens? Do you offer additional training besides the orientation?

JC: No other training. The teens are supervised closely by the librarian conducting programs during that shift.

How does your administration support you and your volunteer program?

JC: I am the administrator, and I am very supportive. Our township council is also supportive. Each year they host the "Teen Appreciation" Council Meeting. Teens are presented with certificates before the council.

Have you learned anything from working with teens?

JC: I have learned that teens are more mature than most people will give them credit for. Teens love children and love working with them.

What about other library staff members? What kinds of reactions and/or relationships have occurred with the volunteers?

JC: The staff has come to rely on the teen volunteers to monitor the summer reading club program. The staff defers to the volunteers in checking in summer readers.

Why should libraries have a teen volunteer program?

JC: It would assist them in monitoring programs during the summer.

Why do teens like to volunteer at your library?

JC: We have a very open, friendly atmosphere. We show our appreciation for teen efforts. These teens were also once members of the summer reading club, so they want to stay involved with the library. (From e-mail interview, 17 September 2002.)

MARITA RICHARDS, CHILDREN'S SERVICES MANAGER

Allen Public Library, Allen, Texas
http://www.ci.allen.tx.us/library/library.htm

Allen is a suburb of the Dallas/Fort Worth metroplex, with a population of about 55,000. It is a town with lots of young families with children. There are ten elementary schools, two middle schools, one freshman center, and one high school. The school population is estimated to be about 13,000 students. The majority of residents are white, with Hispanics and African Americans making up the two largest minority groups in Allen.

Allen Public Library is one central library with no branches. There are nine professional librarians (some are part-time), and fourteen other employees for support staff duties (some part-time, some full-time). In the Children's Department, there are four people on the staff. Marita Richards serves as the Children's Services Manager. Her staff includes a full-time children's librarian, a part-time children's librarian, and a full-time children's clerk.

Please describe your teen volunteer program.

MR: Each April we advertise in-house and at the middle schools, ninth-grade center, and high school for teen volunteers. We give signs, applications, and announcements to the school librarians for use at their schools. Applications are also available at the library.

Teens must have completed sixth grade to apply. We have found that if they are any younger than that, they are just not ready to volunteer. (We have home-school kids volunteer as well.) Teens must be willing to work two-hour shifts once a week. These time slots are in two-hour increments. We have a schedule of times for them to work. The schedule is Monday to Friday in the mornings and early afternoons on Monday through Thursday.

During their shift, they will help register children for the Summer Reading Club, give out prizes for the reading the children have done, make posters advertising summer programs, make crafts to be given out at programs, or assist the librarian at a specific program. If teens are especially interested in helping with preschool story time, they sign up to work Friday morning. During the summer we have one session per week of preschool story time. The teens basically do the program. I select the theme of the story time, the stories, the finger plays, the songs, etc., and the teens pick out the part they want to do. It seems to work well. The teens who do this program are enthusiastic and enjoy the preschool age. We rehearse the story time the week before we do it.

The teens also help at big programs such as our craft programs. About seven tables are set up with crafts for the children to do, and the teens are there to assist the children with the craft. We also have an annual carnival with game booths set up in our meeting room and outdoor courtyard. The teens work the game booths and hand out little prizes of candy, little toys, and hand stamps, etc. Usually after the carnival, we have our teen appreciation lunch, usually pizza.

These teens basically just work in the summer, but during school vacations we often have programs for preschool and elementary children and we call some of our previous teen volunteers to help. For example, we have an annual Trick or Treat at Puppet Town on October 31. We decorate "houses" (large cardboard boxes) as puppet homes. Children come to the library to trick or treat at the puppet houses and receive little items—candy, stickers, grab bags, free paperback books, etc. The teens work the "houses" for us.

We have a Teen Volunteer orientation meeting each year the week before the Summer Reading program starts. The teens are strongly urged to attend. We explain their duties and the programs with which they will be helping. We do not conduct formal one-on-one interviews. Time and staff does not permit us to interview, and we have always felt that the teens are volunteering because of service reasons or interest in the library. Many do volunteer work in the summer for National Honor Society hours or Scout project hours.

We have been doing these same procedures for the entire time I have been here (more than eight years). We have modified things a little each year when we find something works better than something we have been doing. I am in charge of the teens, but the children's clerk has taken over some of the daily duties. She works very closely with the teens, trying to assign tasks they would enjoy and which would best suit their interests. On the teen application, they can list interests such as art, puppetry, playing a musical instrument, etc.

The teens sign in each time they work. We have a notebook with each teen's own sheet where they record the date and time they worked and the activities they did that day.

We issue a teen volunteer certificate and a teen volunteer evaluation to each teen at the end of the summer. The evaluation verifies the number of hours they worked and lists the duties they performed. These duties include: helping with summer reading club registration and record-keeping, assisting at story time, special art assignments, craft preparation, special programs such as the craft program or carnival, and others.

What is your education and experience?

MR: I received my Masters in Library Science in 1976 from the University of North Texas. My experience in libraries includes all areas—reference, cataloging, and children's work. I have worked for many years as a reference librarian at several libraries. This is my second position as a Children's Librarian supervisor. I have been at Allen as Children's Services Manager for eight and a half years. I have seen Allen grow and the library expand its services, hours, and collection. We are in the process of planning and building a new library with groundbreaking to take place in the spring of 2003.

The teen volunteer program was in place when I arrived and has grown ever since. This year we had forty-five teens help us for a total of 912 hours. The teens worked for ten weeks. We try to limit the number of teen volunteers to about thirty, but there are always so many applications at the deadline, that we manage to squeeze them in and find enough for all to do. However, there are days toward the end of the summer that we have to find things for the teens to do, but we just look ahead and have them prepare crafts and name tags for the fall programs we will be doing.

What is your favorite part of working with teen volunteers?

MR: I enjoy working with the teens. We have had very few discipline problems over the years. Minor things have occurred such as proper attire to wear when volunteering, or teens going over to Wendy's when their shift ends instead of waiting for a parent to pick them up. Sometimes a teen is not interested in working because it was Mom's idea to volunteer at the library. These teens tend to weed themselves out of the program.

The teens are fully supervised but do tend to get noisy. Overall, it has been a good opportunity to work with youth. Some teens have used their library volunteer experience on job applications. We get many repeat teen volunteers. Some teens have volunteered three years in a row.

Why do teens want to volunteer at your library?

MR: I think teens like to work here because we give them an opportunity to do a variety of things and use their skills, such as art. A different volunteer job is shelf reading. Teens can sign up to read a designated area of shelves on a regular basis. The adult services desk handles this job. The Children's Department manages the summer teen volunteer program. There is a booklet published annually listing opportunities to volunteer in the county. There are other places for teens to volunteer. The library has been listed in this booklet many times.

How would describe your managerial style? What qualities make a good teen supervisor?

MR: I like the team concept of management. Everyone has a chance to contribute and have a voice in the program. One quality of a good teen supervisor is patience. You have to remember you are dealing with teens and they can be "up" one day and "down" the next. (If you are a parent of a teen, then you can understand and appreciate that statement.) The children's clerk and I are mothers of teens. The children's clerk tries to communicate with the teens and find their interests and direct that interest into a project that we need to do.

What have you learned from the teens you supervise? What have they learned?

MR: A few of the teens over the years have thanked me for the chance to volunteer at the library. Some think libraries are a "cool" place. Hopefully, the teens have learned responsibility, pride in their work, the opportunity to begin developing job skills, and making new friends.

How does your administration support the program?

MR: Our library director is very supportive of the teen volunteer program.

How do you recognize your volunteers?

MR: We recognize our teens with a certificate, an evaluation, and a teen lunch. Some years we have featured them in a local newspaper article. They also love candy.

What qualities make a good volunteer?

MR: Our application states that the teen must be willing to work two hours a week, be dependable, and like working with children. They must be willing to try to do new tasks. They should be dependable and mature, twelve or more years old, to work at the library.

How does the rest of the library respond to the teens?

MR: The rest of the library staff accepts the teen volunteers. In years past, some of the teens would work in the children's work area. However, this room is shared by other staff members, particularly cataloguers who need quiet, and teens love to talk. Therefore, we have moved much of their work out to the public area of the children's department. That is the only problem we have had with staff and teens.

Why should libraries have teen volunteer programs?

MR: Libraries need teen volunteer programs to let the teens know they are welcome at the library. The future of the library profession depends on the next generation. Perhaps a teen who has volunteered at the library might later realize that the library is a profession in which he or she could be interested as a career.

How would you improve your program?

MR: Each year the children's staff reviews the teen volunteer program and we discuss the ways to improve it. We are thinking of redoing the teen volunteer schedule next year so it will better accommodate our crowds at peak times in the children's department. (From e-mail interview, 24 September 2002.)

Sydna Wexler, Young Adult Librarian

Broward County Public Library, Ft. Lauderdale, Florida
www.broward.org/library

Broward County Main Library, located in downtown Ft. Lauderdale, is the main library of a large county library system with thirty-seven branches. This eight-story public library serves a diverse urban community. In recent years, there has been a rise in the Hispanic population and an influx of people from Caribbean countries. Their collection development profile reflects the population shift with increased materials in Spanish and Creole. According to the 2000–2001 Annual Report, the library budget is $40 million. At present, the Main Library has 183 employees. In the Youth Services Department, the staff consists of a department head, assistant head of Youth Services, two Librarian IIs, a graduate intern, and a library clerk. In the future, positions will be filled for two Librarian I positions. Sydna Wexler is designated as the Young Adult Librarian.

What is your background? How did you become interested in serving teens?

SW: My structured educational goals have always been centered on reading. I have a B.A. in liberal arts, a master's degree in English, and a master's in library science from the University of South Florida in 1997. My academic background shaped my ongoing professional goal as a young adult librarian—planning and working with teens to develop innovative YA programs.

My initial experience with teen volunteers, at the Davie Cooper City Library in Davie, Florida, from 1994 to 1999, was highly rewarding. The teen advisory board was composed of teens from various Asian countries (i.e., Taiwan, Japan, India, and Korea). They organized and planned an Asian New Year program that won the Betty Davis Miller Award for outstanding teen program in 1999. At the Main Library, I had the opportunity to assist our teen advisory board with two major multicultural teen-generated programs. In honor of Caribbean Heritage month, a Caribbean Festival was the outcome of the creative efforts of our teen volunteers who were from the Caribbean countries of Jamaica, Haiti, Trinidad, and Grenada. Teen storytelling, craft projects, and a food-tasting table were highlights of this successful program.

The summer library kickoff program (June 16, 2001), Fiesta Fantastica, was an ideal opportunity to focus on the cultural heritage of our Hispanic community. Fiesta Fantastica incorporated bilingual teen storytelling, folk dancing, and Hispanic craft tables. For further information about the Caribbean Festival and Fiesta Fantastica, refer to my article in *Voice of Youth Advocates* (October, 2001, pp. 247–49).

What's your favorite thing about working with teen volunteers?

SW: The perks of supervising teen volunteers are many. A positive aspect is their boundless creative energy and determination to implement their teen programs.

What's your least favorite thing?

SW: I always dislike counseling a teen who has repeatedly violated our volunteer guidelines.

Describe an instance where volunteering really made a difference in a teen's life.

SW: Two years ago, a teen volunteer who recently immigrated from Haiti was experiencing overwhelming personal and academic problems. Through the course of the year, I discovered Chrislene's talents as a singer and poet. Her self-esteem soared when she received special recognition at our Teen Talent Show. Last year, Chrislene graduated from high school and received a scholarship to pursue her career in music.

What have you learned from the teens themselves or from working with them?

SW: I have acquired a determination never to dismiss a potential program idea as an impossibility. Also, the teens have a sense of pride when they participate and plan an outstanding YA program.

How do you train volunteers? Which methods work best in your situation?

SW: The two-hour mandatory orientations, scheduled in the fall, winter, and summer, offer an initial overview of volunteer duties, special projects, and guidelines. Teen Advisory Board (TAB) members discuss eligibility for TAB nomination.

A tour of the Youth Services Department incorporates a "hands-on" training session about the role of teen volunteers in terms of maintaining order in the Youth Services Department. Follow-up is essential with all new volunteers. The best method is pairing a small group of new teen volunteers with experienced volunteers.

How does your administration and/or supervisor support your efforts?

SW: The support for teen programs is reflected in the approval of budget requests for YA programs, which are sponsored by the Friends of the Fort Lauderdale Library. The recognition of the teen volunteers at the annual volunteer awards program reinforces the crucial role that our teens play in the daily functioning in the Youth Services Department.

Can anyone volunteer? What if someone attends a volunteer orientation and then doesn't show up? Do you have schedules/commitments from the teens?

SW: Our current policy indicates that teens, thirteen to eighteen years old, can volunteer in the Youth Services Department after completing an orientation. If a volunteer cannot attend the orientation, special arrangements are provided for a make-up training session. In terms of scheduling, teen volunteers are assigned specific two-hour time slots. If unable to volunteer at the assigned day and time, teens are required to contact a Youth Services librarian.

What qualities make a good volunteer?

SW: An ideal teen volunteer is reliable and completes an assigned duty within a reasonable amount of time.

What do you expect from your volunteers?

SW: All teens have a clear understanding of volunteer guidelines after the initial orientation. A list of rules is discussed and must be signed by new volunteers. The signed guidelines are retained in their respective volunteer folders as an acknowledgment of the rules.

What qualities make a good teen volunteer manager? Do you think all YA librarians could be volunteer managers? Why or why not?

SW: Traditionally, teens have been regarded with suspicion largely on the basis of initial appearance ("outlandish" clothing and body piercings). A prerequisite for a potential young adult librarian is to dispel stereotypes and establish an environment of trust. When working with teens, a YA librarian should have an open-minded, flexible attitude. Also, patience and empathy are essential when responding to this age group. Above all, teens need to be encouraged in creative self-expression.

Which teen volunteer do you remember and why?

SW: At Davie Cooper City Library, Jennifer Rodriguez, the president of the teen advisory board, made a lasting impression of a model teen volunteer and future leader. Jennifer had a versatile range of talents—art, music, and theater. She was instrumental in implementing and assisting at an afternoon creative dramatics program for preteens.

How does the library staff respond to the volunteers and the volunteer program?

SW: I am fortunate to work with youth services librarians who have been highly supportive of the teen volunteers. The extra attention has been reflected by their attendance at events that feature our talented teens. Special incentives have been demonstrated such as appreciation pizza parties. Positive staff reinforcement has been beneficial in terms of the ever-expanding request for volunteering at the Main Library. (From e-mail interview, 20 September 2002.)

MARY MCKINNEY, YOUNG ADULT LIBRARIAN

Tucson-Pima Public Library, Tucson, Arizona
www.library.ci.tucson.az.us

Tucson is located in the southeastern corner of Arizona. Pima County, including the City of Tucson, has a population of around 900,000. The largest portion of Tucson's population is of Anglo descent, with the second largest group claiming Hispanic origins. Average January temperatures range from 38 to 64 degrees while July temperatures average from 74 to 98 degrees. Tucson is a university town. The University of Arizona students have a fluctuating effect on our population each year, and the school is also one of the city's largest employers. Davis Monthan Air Force Base is also located in Tucson, and has a positive effect on Tucson's labor market and economy.

Tucson-Pima Public Library (TPPL) consists of twenty-two city and county locations and a bookmobile. There is a Young Adult Services Committee that meets bimonthly to discuss topics related to teen services. The committee is composed of branch librarians whose responsibilities include teen services. The library has teen nonfiction and fiction collections, teen programming, a teen website, and a teen summer reading program (theme and incentives chosen by teens). The Main Library has an entire "teen only" room on the second floor. The décor and the resources were recommended by teens.

Some branches have teen volunteers all year long, but the majority of the teen volunteers offer their time in the summer. Teens are recruited during the summer to assist with the children's summer reading program. The teens' main responsibility is to get kids started and give them incentives throughout the two months of the program. In 2002, fourteen branches had a total of 176 volunteers. There is not a specific volunteer budget; however, some funds (about $300) are available from the teen summer reading program budget for gifts to thank volunteers at the end of their service.

What is your background? How did you get to be involved with teens and teen volunteers?

MM: I am a former California children's librarian who jumped at the chance to return to Tucson to work with teens.

How do you recognize and reward your volunteers?

MM: To reward and recognize volunteers, many young adult services librarians host parties at the end of the summer. Some librarians have held after-hours events, pizza parties, pajama parties, film fests, and game gigs. Refreshments are a must! Additionally, volunteers are given little treats such as mugs, pens, pencils, and candies as well as a certificate of thanks.

How do you train and orient your volunteers? Which methods work best in your situation?

MM: Some librarians have orientation/training sessions with their whole group of volunteers, but others prefer to do so one at a time. It usually depends on the number of volunteers a librarian is supervising. If handouts are given to the volunteers, it works best to verbally review everything on those handouts with the teens. This way, you know that you covered information on the dress code, for example, and you will be less likely to have a problem during the course of their volunteer time.

What do you expect from your volunteers?

MM: I expect volunteers to have as much fun as they can, to encourage the kids to keep up their reading, to keep supplies organized, arrive on time and notify me when they are unable to volunteer, and to ask questions about anything!

What makes a teen succeed as a volunteer? What qualities do you look for?

MM: Enthusiastic, personable, and outgoing teens who like to work with young children will succeed as volunteers at TPPL.

Which teen volunteer do you remember most and why?

MM: David is one volunteer I remember most. He was here the first year I came to my current branch. The kids loved him! He would occasionally wear his football jersey from his high school team, and he really drew the kids in and made them feel great about their reading. He was well liked by the female teen volunteers, too, of course!

Michelle is another teen who shined. She participated in a panel presentation on teen volunteers at the Public Library Association conference in Phoenix in 2002. Her poise, charm, and confidence are amazing.

Megan was a golden volunteer from day one. She has volunteered for the last three years. She is enthusiastic, dependable, smart, and invaluable. She is such a pro that she can train other teen volunteers.

What's your favorite part about supervising teens? What is your least favorite?

MM: My favorite part about supervising teens is getting to know them. They have great ideas and an endless supply of energy.

What qualities make a successful teen volunteer manager?

MM: A successful teen volunteer manager is organized, appreciative, and patient.

Why should libraries hire teen volunteers? What's in it for them?

MM: Libraries should hire teen volunteers because . . .

1. teens want to volunteer.
2. teens can take on work that will give library staff ability to focus on priority work.
3. teens in the library make the library more appealing to other teens.
4. staff and customers can develop positive relationships with them.

Teens gain experience filling out applications, undergoing job training, and practicing job-related responsibilities such as dress codes and punctuality. It is also helpful to teens to be able to list their volunteer experience on their resumes.

How does the staff respond to the teens? How do they support the teen volunteer program?

MM: Library staff assists in training and answering questions the teens might have during their volunteer experience. Sometimes staff works alongside the teens for training or assistance during busy moments.

One librarian asked the rest of the staff at her branch to write on a piece of paper why they liked having the teen volunteers at their library. She gathered all the responses and read them aloud to her group of teen volunteers. Great idea! (From e-mail interview, 30 September 2002.)

Kimberly Paone, Young Adult Librarian

Elizabeth Public Library, Elizabeth, New Jersey
www.njpublib.org

Elizabeth has approximately 120,000 residents. Adjacent to Newark, New Jersey, it is about twenty-five minutes from midtown Manhattan. Elizabeth is an urban, multicultural environment. There is a very large Hispanic community (both Spanish and Portuguese speakers) as well as a large African-American community. Elizabeth has the largest public high school in the state, with more than 3,500 students—located three blocks from the main library. The Free Public Library of Elizabeth has a main library and three small branches, with a staff of approximately fifty employees.

The Teen Department at the Elizabeth Public Library offers a different kind of teen volunteer program—one teen at a time. This opportunity is available to young adults who have been ordered by a court to volunteer somewhere in the community as well as teens who need to fulfill a school requirement for community service hours. Kimberly Paone is the lone staff member of the department, so she works with each teen until volunteer hours are completed, then accepts another teen volunteer until his or her hours are completed, and so on. She partners with the area public and private high schools, the Union County Juvenile Probation Department, and the Elizabeth Municipal Court, which all refer teens to the library for volunteer work. While the schools generally assign small amounts of time to volunteer (two to twenty hours), the courts assign between thirty and a hundred hours of required service.

Kimberly accepts volunteers year-round, but none are referred from the schools during the summer, of course. Teen volunteers perform a variety of tasks after receiving a tour of the library on their first day. Duties include shelving books and straightening shelves, filing and typing, creating displays, and evaluating websites that might be of interest to teen library users. There are several requirements that the teens must complete before finishing their volunteer service, however. Each teen must get a library card, become familiar with the online catalog and at least one subscription database, read at least one book, and attend at least one teen program. Nine students have completed 178 hours of community service since early 2001, five of whom were court-ordered volunteers.

Do you interview? Why or why not? How do you decide whom you will hire?

KP: Students are interviewed before I agree to take them on. I have an understanding with all of the agencies that I can refuse kids if I so choose (although I have yet to do so). When I interview them, I just try to get a feel for their level of cooperativeness and what I think they're going to be able to handle intellectually. Sometimes the teens I get have trouble even with the simplest tasks such as alphabetizing/shelving, so I like to know what challenges we're going to face from the outset. I pretty much take everyone.

What characteristics are you looking for? Have you determined what kinds of kids make the best volunteers?

KP: The best characteristics are good reading ability, sharp alphabetizing, attention to detail, being able to follow directions, good work ethic, punctuality, and consistency as far as showing up when they're scheduled. I have had kids that possess all of these qualities, kids that possess none of them, kids who tried hard to compensate for not having them, and kids who frankly didn't care. The best volunteer is eager to help with whatever task is put in front of him, doesn't mind keeping himself busy (maybe straightening shelves) while waiting for direction (if I'm with a patron when a task is completed), and has all the qualities mentioned above. They're rare, but I've had at least one from the court and more than one from schools.

You take court-ordered teens. How does this impact the program? Is there any concern about these kids from staff? Do you notice any difference between the court-ordered and the community-service teens as far as dependability, completion of tasks, etc.?

KP: The staff doesn't say much about the court-ordered teens, probably because the kids doing community service are introduced as that: kids doing community service. I make no differentiation between the ones from the court and the ones from schools. Also, they know that the kids from the court are nonviolent, first-time offenders (truancy, breaking curfew, riding on the back of a motorcycle without a helmet, etc.), so that probably makes them less scary to the staff. And the kids only work in the Teen Department under my direct supervision. With only a couple of exceptions (see "The Dark Side," chapter 7), the court-ordered kids and the high school-ordered kids are about the same as far as dependability. Most of the court-ordered teens realize that if they screw up they're going to be in a lot more trouble and their next assignment will not be nearly as cushy as the library.

Do you evaluate the volunteers? How?

KP: Both the court and the schools provide me with evaluation forms that I must complete and return after the student has completed his or her hours. I really don't use any other evaluative methods—because I only have one at a time, it's pretty easy to keep track of what he or she has or hasn't done. The criteria that the teens must complete before their service are my own; the schools and the court leave me to my own devices as far as what I have the kids doing. Their evaluations have more to do with punctuality, completion of tasks, etc.

What have you learned from working with teen volunteers?

KP: I think I've had to become more patient. I've learned that some kids need things explained to them in different ways, and sometimes numerous times. What have I learned from "The Dark Side" experiences? Just that we can only do so much. There are kids we cannot help, who will not accept our help. I just try to move on and hope that the next experience will be better.

Any success stories?

KP: Well, some of the first court-ordered volunteers I had last year still stop in on occasion to say hello—I think that's success! These are kids who had never stepped foot in the library before being forced to, and now they come willingly, sometimes to read a magazine, use the computer, check out a book. I had a deaf student in the beginning of this year and that was a challenge for both of us. She doesn't speak much and I have very limited sign language—we taught each other quite a bit working with notes and body language and lots of laughter. She has turned up from time to time for teen programs. I know that working in the library gave her a real sense of accomplishment. It's funny how some kids are genuinely sad when their time is up! (From e-mail interview, 15 August 2002.)

Note: Kimberly Paone won the 2002 New York Times *Librarian Award for outstanding public service. Four teens from the Elizabeth Public Library nominated her for the award, stating that she helps teens feel welcome in the library. Not only do the teens learn how to find information and books to read, but Kimberly provides guidance with life decisions and daily anxieties. Her efforts with teenage patrons and volunteers are duly recognized with this award.*

Successful Teen Volunteer Programs

LITERACY DAYCAMP

Berkeley Public Library, Berkeley, California
www.infopeople.org/bpl
Coordinator: Francisca Goldsmith, Teen Services Coordinator

Literacy Daycamp is a collaborative effort between the three departments of the Berkeley Public Library: Children's Services, Teen Services, and the adult literacy program, Berkeley Reads. Berkeley Reads is a library program that provides tutors for adult learners who need to improve their literacy skills. Literacy Daycamp complements Berkeley Reads by offering tutoring to the adult learners' school-aged children by specially trained teen tutors. The camp runs two days a week for six weeks during the summer. Each camp day is broken into two one-hour segments: the first hour focuses on academic curriculum designed by the literacy staff, and the second hour features a program or activity sponsored by the Children's Services staff that reinforces these learning objectives. The teen volunteers tutor the children during the first part and assist with the program choices during the second part. In addition, the tutors devote time during each camp day for pleasure reading together in the children's section of the library.

Recruitment for this program is done during spring booktalking presentations at area schools. A special effort is made to recruit teens who are fluent in a second language, since many of the neighborhood children are children of immigrant parents. The staff emphasizes that they are seeking teens with good study habits to be role models for the younger students and that academic excellence is not a prerequisite for volunteering. The teens complete applications and must attend two training sessions with instruction provided by the literacy staff and teen librarians. During these training sessions, they learn about teaching methods, learning styles, the importance of reading, library policies, and how to interact with the children. In addition, they help the Children's Department staff plan the curriculum-based program, even conducting some of the programs themselves. In the past, the teen tutors have presented craft programs, bookmaking projects, and theater experiences. The volunteers also help the campers complete their summer reading program while at the library.

The costs for the program include the staff time of a literacy office assistant, the literacy coordinator, and teen and children's librarians who participate in the program as part of their regular duties. Teen Services provides funds from their program budget for the training lunch and some snacks for the campers. Children's Services provides funds for performers from their program budget, and the Literacy Department supplies art, curriculum, and training materials. Local merchants donate funds for additional snacks for the campers and tutors.

The teen tutors are recognized for their efforts in several ways. They are invited to a party on the last day to celebrate the success of the program and to recognize the efforts of both campers and tutors. They also receive certificates of appreciation. The neighborhood teens are faithful participants in this program. They attend each day-camp session (a thirty-two-hour time commitment) that includes training, evaluation, and twice weekly camping days. The returning volunteers are the best recruiters and quickly become advocates for the program. An added benefit to this cooperative program is the appreciation and respect that has arisen between the three library departments. By working together, they have become partners combining their knowledge and resources for the benefit of the community. (For further information, see Goldsmith's *VOYA* article, February 2001, pp. 408–9.)

Berkeley Public Library
Literacy Daycamp
Teen Volunteer Tutor Application
2001

Name _____

Address _____
             street   city   zip

E-mail address (if applicable) _____

Home Phone _____ Parent/Guardian work phone _____

Grade and school you attend _____

Languages in which you are fluent _____

Physical limitations _____

Previous work experience, volunteer or paid

_____

_____

Skills, hobbies and special interests

_____

_____

Reasons for wanting to volunteer at Berkeley Public Library

_____

_____

Your signature _____ Date _____

Parent/Guardian signature _____

Berkeley Public Library
Literacy Daycamp
Teen Volunteer Tutor
Job Description
2001

This will be the fifth year Berkeley Public Library has offered the opportunity for summer academic enrichment to children whose families participate in the library's adult literacy program. The daycamp meets two afternoons a week, at West Branch (1125 University Avenue) for six weeks, from mid-June (after the BUSD school year ends) through July. Teen Volunteer Tutors work with the individual campers to improve reading skills, interest and academic readiness. This program is cosponsored by Berkeley Public Library's Literacy Office, Children's Services, and Teen Services.

Teen Tutors are provided a mandatory seven-hour training that includes information about working at the city agency of the Library, as well as learning and teaching techniques. There are two opportunities for training this spring. Each tutor may attend sessions on April 9, 11 and 13, or the all-day make-up session on April 28. In either case, the tutor must complete all 7 hours of training in order to volunteer with the Daycamp program this summer.

Potential tutors do not need to excel in school themselves, but they must have an interest in reading, children and public service.

In addition to academic skills, part of each daycamp session is spent "doing something fun," including participating in craft programs, enjoying visiting performers, etc. Teen Volunteer Tutors assist in – and can help initiate – producing the "fun" element of the day as well as in the academic portion.

If you have questions about whether you are well suited to this community service opportunity, please contact the Senior Librarian for Teen Services, Francisca Goldsmith at the Berkeley Public Library.

KAST: Kids As Storytellers

Monona Public Library, Monona, Wisconsin
www.scls.lib.wi.us/monona
Coodinator: Karen Wendt, Young Adult Librarian

Kids As Storytellers is a small group of teens who work together to perform for preschoolers and young children by reading picture books, singing songs, creating and performing flannelboard stories, doing fingerplays, and putting on skits. Youth in grades five through eight who are a part of Kids As Storytellers reinforce their reading skills and confidence, gain insight into performance situations, broaden their appreciation of children's literature, and have loads of fun.

The Kids As Storytellers (KAST) program was designed to increase the involvement of middle school youth with literature in new ways—as tellers, not just readers. During the initial training session during late May or early June, the participants are given tips on choosing and reading aloud picture books to a group of children, including resources to find stories. They also are introduced to various storytelling techniques, including fingerplays, prop stories, flannelboard stories, Reader's Theater, and traditional oral storytelling. In addition, the training session is the time to get organized about what they will do the first week of the summer story times. Not many teens show up for the training, but it doesn't really matter to Karen Wendt, since she often waits until the day of the program for planning.

KAST members are not preregistered. During the summer of 2002, Karen started the summer with three interested girls. By the end of the summer, she had fifteen teens who were coming on a regular basis, with five to eight showing up each week. KAST was mostly girls, but two boys started coming toward the end and stated their interest in doing it next year. Because she does not use registration, Karen tries to have five or six different types of stories ready to handle the various number of KAST members who come each week. She decides which stories to use in the morning when the teens arrive. This is a fly-by-the-seat-of-the-pants method that others might want to do differently, perhaps by having teens sign up and commit to the program ahead of time, but it works for Karen and her group.

During the summer of 2002, they used a technique called "stories on stage" or "instant theater." Karen tells a story to the group of KAST, usually a familiar folktale with a simple plot, lots of action, and a flexible number of characters. After telling the story, the KAST group works out who will be which characters of the story, sometimes including inanimate characters. Then they "tell" the story. They practice the story two or three times, editing and rearranging it as they go. Sometimes the story is in complete dialogue and sometimes they choose to add a narrator or even puppets and other props.

KAST members come to the library story room in the children's area at 9:30 a.m. Each week, the group has only one hour to prepare before the children arrive at 10:30

to attend the story time program. Karen opens the program and reads one or two books or tells a story. KAST performs one to three skits, depending on the enthusiasm and skill of that particular group. Karen fills in the rest of the thirty- to forty-five-minute program with short stories, songs, fingerplays, or books, and the closing. Since she runs it as a drop-in program, sometimes she doesn't know how many teen volunteers will show up that day, but she has a variety of options planned to fit any number of performers.

KAST volunteers are allowed to come to the final pool party (a reading incentive for all who enter the reading part of the summer program), and invited to an end-of-the-summer Junior Volunteer party. They get coupons from area businesses and a letter stating their community service hours. The 2002 group was so excited about the program that three to five of them are continuing to help tell stories for the fall family Night Stories series.

There is always a ready audience of children for the KAST performers. It is publicized in the summer reading program flyers that go out in May to students in all classes of grades K–8. It is advertised in the paper, on posters and brochures in the library, and in the Community Recreation Guide published by the Recreation Department in March. In addition, brochures are handed out at a community Family Night sponsored by the school district. Children love watching KAST performances, teens love creating them, and Karen Wendt loves facilitating the process.

Some stories used by KAST during their performances:

Brown Bear, Brown Bear by Bill Martin (Henry Holt, 1983)
From Head to Toe by Eric Carle (HarperCollins, 1997)
George and Martha by James Marshall (Houghton Mifflin, 1972)
The Great Ball Game by Joseph Bruchac (Dial, 1994)
Greedy Old Fat Man by Paul Galdone (Houghton Mifflin, 1983)
I Am the Dog, I Am the Cat by Donald Hall (Dial, 1994)
Katy No Pocket by Emmy Payne, illustrator H. A. Rey (Houghton Mifflin, 1944)
Mixed Up Chameleon by Eric Carle (HarperCollins, 1984)
Monster Under My Bed by Suzanne Gruber (Troll, 1997)
Polar Bear, Polar Bear by Bill Martin (Henry Holt, 1991)
Queen's Holiday by Margaret Wild, illustrator Sue O'Loughlin (Orchard, 1992)
Gingerbread Man
Henny Penny
Three Billy Goats Gruff

(NOTE: For a similar program pairing teens with children at story times, see appendix B for the article "KidWorks Is Kid-Made," reprinted from *VOYA*, October 2003.)

Kids As Storytellers

Introduction to Kids As Storytellers (KAST)

Kids as Storytellers participants will have the opportunity to perform in Reader's Theatre skits or tell short stories to children ages 2 to 10 years old. Practices are held from 9:30-10:30 a.m. and Storytime programs are held 10:30-11:15 a.m. Wednesday mornings from June 12 to July 31. We will be in the Forum Room at the library.

If you are interested in learning more about this opportunity, come to the June 5 introductory session, 6:30 to 7:45 p.m. There is no obligation to be a KAST member if you attend the *Introduction to Kids As Storytellers* program on June 12.

If you think you would like to participate, please complete the form below and return it to the Monona Public Library. Mark it *attention Karen*. You can also call Karen at 222-6127, or drop by at 9:30 a.m. on any Wednesday morning between June 12 and July 31.

....

KIDS AS STORYTELLERS

Please print clearly.

NAME: _____ MALE/FEMALE _____

AGE: _____ GRADE: _____ SCHOOL: _____

PHONE NUMBER: _____

ADDRESS: _____

☐ I cannot attend the program on June 12, but I am interested. I will call Karen at 222-6127 to make arrangements for a brief training or will drop in on Wednesday morning, _____.
(date)

PARENT SIGNATURE: _____ DATE: _____

Summer Teen Volunteer Program

Paso Robles Public Library, Paso Robles, California
www.rain.org/~prplynx
Coodinator: Julie Dahlen, Children's Services Librarian

At the Paso Robles Public Library, summer teen volunteers assist with conducting the summer Reading Program each year. They register children, distribute prizes, assist with activities, and shelve books. Older teens may be assigned to other areas in the library such as book mending, computer assistance, or even circulation. Summer Teen Volunteers must be at least thirteen years old. Teens wishing to work in the regular Volunteer Associates Program for the library must be at least sixteen because of the volunteer autonomy and labor laws. There are usually eight to ten teens participating during a seven-week session. Some teens have volunteered at the library for three or more years.

Teens must complete an application and list references. The volunteer coordinator calls references and forwards applications to Julie Dahlen. She interviews candidates, asking such questions as: What does it mean to behave in a professional manner? What would you do if your friends wanted to sit with you at the desk, use the phone, etc.? What experience have you had working with children? There is a "Volunteer Academy" workshop in mid-June for all children's services volunteers in the library (and any other interested library volunteer or staff person). Teens are asked to attend at the time they successfully complete their interviews. They also receive on-the-job training, and the volunteer coordinator provides a general library orientation. The Volunteer Academy is not particularly geared toward teens, but is aimed at increasing the professional competence of full-time adult volunteers. Workshops are offered for each library department, and participants can "graduate." They are honored at the end of the academy series.

Evaluations of teens' work performances are done informally. Younger teens always work with an adult volunteer or Julie, who monitor performance as they go. Older teens are assigned to a supervising staff person. Julie's biggest problem is communicating the expectation of commitment she has for these teens. "Many this summer have informed me at the last minute that they will miss several of their shifts due to vacations, camps, and the like. Library staff recently brainstormed some ideas to encourage teens to take the assignment more seriously. Occasionally, parents can be problematic in their zeal to have their child work in the library—in spite of their child's lack of interest. I have become better at screening out these situations before offering the teen an assignment." One new idea is to keep a mailing list of teens who ask about volunteering throughout the year. Usually, Julie makes applications available during the month of May and hires in June, which is a pretty narrow window. Keeping a list of interested teens might enable them to recruit teens who truly are committed to volunteering.

Teen volunteers are recognized by displaying their photographs in the library throughout the summer, and their names are published in local media. At the end of the program, they are given a small gift, a certificate, and a pizza party. According to Julie, the benefits of teen volunteers far outweigh the disadvantages. "I enjoy working with teens because of their exuberance and because I feel the experience they are gaining is valuable. The downside? Attendance, the need to oversee their work constantly, and inexperience." Her advice for other teen volunteer supervisors? Create a "volunteer buddy system" in which an experienced adult volunteer shares a shift with a teen. The more experienced volunteer can help keep the teen on task, and can cover a shift if a teen does not report to duty.

Welcome!

Welcome to the Paso Robles Library Summer Teen Volunteer Program. You are now an important part of an enthusiastic and dedicated team. We appreciate your commitment to the library and we look forward to a mutually rewarding experience.

This handbook contains general information as well as specific instructions for job assignments. Feel free to make notes in it and be sure to add any updates you may receive.

Brief History of the Volunteer Programs

The Volunteer Associates Program was instituted in 1995 to help the library staff make full use of its beautiful new building. Starting with only a handful of volunteers, the program has grown to become one of California's most innovative experiments in volunteerism, with nearly 100 trained volunteers providing a wealth of talent and expertise to the Paso Robles Public Library. Summer Teen Volunteers, in particular, have been a vital component in the smooth operation of the Summer Reading Program.

Eligibility

The minimum age for a Summer Teen Volunteer is 13. Those who are 16 or older may also be eligible for the Volunteer Associates Program, which offers volunteer opportunities throughout the library.

Time Commitment

Four hours per week are required for the duration of the Summer Reading Program. Exceptions to the time commitment are made on a case-by-case basis.

Record Keeping

Volunteers keep track of their time on time sheets, which are kept in the Volunteer office. Before beginning your shift, record the date and time you started. After completing your shift, record the time out and the total hours given. There is also a column to record the work you did and any comments you have. At the end of each month, the time sheets are tallied and the information is submitted to the City Librarian for statistical use.

Training

The library staff is dedicated to excellence in training. Much of the task-specific training is on-the-job, under the guidance of a designated supervisor.

Service with a Smile

Courtesy is highly valued by the City organization and customer service at the library will very often begin with you. As a library volunteer, you are an ambassador of the city to its residents and a welcoming smile and hospitable attitude are important. To this end, maintain a professional attitude, but be courteous. Always dress in business attire, yet comfortably, and wear shoes suitable for safety.

Dependability

Courtesy on the job extends to coworkers. If you do not keep to your scheduled days and times, you are negatively impacting staff and coworkers. If you are unable to report for work at your regularly scheduled day and time, you are responsible for finding a qualified replacement.

Confidentiality

As a volunteer, you may have access to personal information about library patrons, other volunteers, or city staff. This information may include addresses, phone numbers, birth dates, or materials a patron has checked out, reserved, or has overdue. All information about library patrons or personnel, including fellow volunteers, is confidential. Never divulge any information about customers' reading preferences or library records to anyone, including family members, law enforcement officers, teachers, etc. Volunteers are held to the same standards as are paid staff in maintaining confidentiality. This also applies to information regarding library security.

Library Etiquette

Remember libraries are quiet places. Many of your friends and acquaintances will be pleased to see you at the library as you volunteer. If they want to chat, please take them into the lobby or outside for visiting. Remember, while inside the library you are on duty.

Public telephones are available for customers to use. Please make yourself familiar with their locations so you can refer customers to them. Your personal calls are to be kept to a minimum.

Usually, food and beverages are not allowed in the library; they are allowed in the break room and outside the library. Occasionally, exceptions will be made for special programs and events.

Final Thoughts

It cannot be stressed enough: whether you work with the public or behind the scenes, your participation in the Paso Robles Summer Teen Volunteer Program is truly appreciated and your contribution to the Paso Robles community is invaluable. Thank you!

The Paso Robles Public Library

City of El Paso De Robles
"The Pass of the Oaks"
1000 Spring Street
Paso Robles, CA 93446

APPLICATION FOR THE SUMMER TEEN VOLUNTEER LIBRARY PROGRAM

The Paso Robles City Library Summer Teen Volunteer Program is a 7-week commitment to voluntary service.

DEADLINE TO FILE APPLICATION: (date)
Please print neatly.

Last Name:_____First:_____Middle Initial:____

Street Address:_____City:_____Zip Code:_____

Home Phone:_____

Do you speak a second language? Yes____ No____. If yes, my second language is

_____.

EXTRA CURRICULAR ACTIVITIES

_____

_____

_____

List any other skills or interests (please describe):

_____

_____

_____

REFERENCES

Name_____Phone #_____

Name_____Phone #_____

Name_____Phone #_____

In order to best serve the public and program, it is necessary for volunteers to be available for a definite time commitment. Please *list* the hours (a.m. and p.m.) you are available:

DAYS	TIMES YOU CAN WORK
MON (between 9:30 am & 8:00 pm):	
TUES (between 9:30 am & 8:00 pm):	
WED (between 11:30 am & 8:00 pm):	
THUR (between 11:30 am & 8:00 pm):	
FRI (between 9:30 am & 5:00 pm):	

I agree to comply with the City of Paso Robles Library rules and procedures to the best of my ability. I agree to respect the confidential nature of information I may obtain. I also agree to participate in orientation and training as is required by my assignment.

Volunteer applicant's signature:_____ Date:_____

Parent/Guardian's signature: _____Date:_____

Please note that there is a limited number of positions available. Qualified applicants will be called for an interview. The selection process also involves a reference check and fingerprinting. Thank you for your interest.

Greetings from the Children's Services Librarian

Thank you for your interest in the Paso Robles Public Library's Summer Teen Volunteer Program. Hundreds of young children take part in the Summer Reading Program and our enthusiastic teen volunteers are a vital component in keeping the program running smoothly. Keep in mind that volunteering for the library is like having a job. We count on you to be here when scheduled. Please read the following information on selection and orientation procedures. If you are able to commit to a 4-hour shift each week for our 7-week program, fill out the attached application and return it to the library.

Application: Please be as complete as you can, and remember, neatness counts! Being a Teen Volunteer requires much writing and record keeping, so be sure to show us your best work. References are important as well. List adults who can attest to your skills in working with the public (especially children), your organizational skills, and your dependability. They will be called to verify your eligibility.

Interview: If, through your application and references, you demonstrate appropriate talent and enthusiasm for the position, I will call you for an interview. Professional attire and a friendly, energetic attitude are important characteristics that I will look for in the interview phase.

Scheduling and Orientation: Once accepted into the Program, you will be assigned a shift. Then your orientation to the Library will be scheduled with Suzanne Ontiveros, Volunteer Associates Program Coordinator.

Training: I will provide on-the-job training.

Benefits of being a Summer Teen Volunteer are many. They include working in pleasant surroundings, interacting with friendly staff and other volunteers, developing new skills, helping people, and sharing your own knowledge. Perhaps most importantly, however, Summer Teen Volunteers have the satisfaction of knowing they are providing a much-needed, much appreciated service to the children of our community.

Best of luck to you!

Julie Dahlen, Children's Services Librarian

Teen Library Corps (TLC)

Wake Forest Public Library, Wake Forest, North Carolina
www.co.wake.nc.us/library
Coordinator: Jane R. Deacle, Young Adult Librarian

The Teen Library Corps at Wake Forest Public Library offers young adults aged twelve to sixteen the opportunity to volunteer in the library and assist staff members with various activities and tasks. The purposes of the program:

- Encourage young adults to come to the library.
- Provide a venue for young adults to volunteer.
- Allow young adults to learn more about the workings of the library.
- Give library staff help with day-to-day tasks and allow staff to establish a rapport with the young adult population.
- Give young adults the experience of working in a job that requires them to show up at a specified time and work a set number of hours.

APPLICATION PROCESS

After each young adult completes and returns an application, he or she is contacted to come in for an interview. The interview, which lasts fifteen to twenty minutes, is with the coordinator of the program or a designated staff member. The purpose of the interview is twofold: to meet the candidate and assess maturity, and to provide the opportunity to participate in an interview process. (In the five years that Jane Deacle has been involved in the program, there has been only one applicant who was not accepted into the program after the interview process.) After the interview, the young adult is given a T-shirt and a work schedule, based on his or her availability and openings in the library. Teen volunteers usually work two times a week in one-and-a-half-hour time periods for ten weeks. Generally the schedule is made so that only one teen is volunteering during a specific period.

WHO, WHEN, AND HOW

Teen Library Corps volunteers are either on break from a year-round school program, on summer vacation, being home schooled, or helping after the school day. They are taken into the corps throughout the year in ten-week blocks on a staggered basis, so that staff is not overwhelmed by training a group of ten or twelve teens at one time. Summer provides the largest group of ten to twelve volunteers. During the past year (August 2001 to July 2002), twenty-two young adults volunteered for a total of 432 hours.

The local Junior Woman's Club and Friends of the Wake Forest Public Library underwrite the corps. This sponsorship allows the staff to purchase T-shirts, provide gift certificates to a local bookstore at the completion of ten weeks, and purchase pizza and collage supplies for the end of year pizza/collage party.

Each TLC volunteer is asked to read a book from the young adult collection and either write a report or construct a display spotlighting the book and its author.

DISPLAY POSTER WORKSHOP

Each teen volunteer has the opportunity to attend one of the poster-making workshops offered three times a year. At these workshops, they are shown how to put together a poster to use as part of a library display spotlighting various authors, illustrators, or genres. After the initial instruction, each teen makes a poster from materials prepared for the workshop. Those who complete the workshop are allowed to make poster displays during the time they volunteer.

PIZZA/COLLAGE PARTY

At the end of the summer a pizza/collage party is held for volunteers who have taken part in the TLC program during the past year. The party is usually held on Friday evening after the library closes and lasts for approximately two hours.

The evening begins with pizza, dessert, soft drinks, and conversation—an opportunity for the teens to talk about the books they have read and discuss their volunteer experience. Based on these discussions, the coordinator adds and omits various tasks from the expectations list. For example, when Jane first took over the program, the volunteers shelved picture books. At one of the pizza gatherings, the teens said they did not like shelving picture books, and admitted to just putting the books on the shelves without paying attention to correct order. Therefore, Jane decided to omit picture-book shelving from the list of suggested tasks.

After the pizza and conversation, participants are introduced to the basics of collage-making. Teens are given pieces of foam core board with pre-stamped colorful backgrounds, sheets of paper printed with their names and the author's names from the book they read, and printed copies of their book's cover. There is a variety of media available to include on collages: various types of paper for texture, such as construction, origami, tissue, scrapbook, and cellophane; pictures from magazines, newspapers, and books; various shapes cut from foam and paper; chenille stems; etc. Using a glue gun, teens attach items to their collages until they are satisfied with the finished product. Then they sign their names. The collages are framed and hung in the library.

WHAT DO THEY DO?

The Teen Library Corps members assist the staff with a variety of projects:

- Processing books—attaching genre stickers and various other identification stickers to books.
- Preparing magazines for circulation.
- Packing books that have been weeded from the shelves.

- Preparing posters for displays.
- Helping a staff member shift book collections.
- Pulling books from the shelf for requests from other libraries and preparing them for transit.
- Checking in books sent to the library to fill patrons' requests and placing these books in alphabetical order on the hold shelf.
- Checking library holdings of specific books in preparation for book orders.
- Withdrawing books that have been weeded.
- Cleaning computer screens and keyboards.
- Cutting scrap paper.
- Stuffing brochures.

The following samples of the forms and flyers that Jane uses with the TLC program include her comments as sidebars.

TLC

This is the cover for the notebook where I keep
- roster of present TLC members complete with name, address, phone number, work schedule, and volunteer time period
- time sheet
- post notices of workshops
- a copy of TLC expectations
- a copy of suggested tasks for TLC members – for staff convenience

Logbook

June	Teen Library Corps - Summer 2002							
	Name	Name	Name	Name	Name	Name	Name	Name
1								
2								
3								
4								
5								
6								
7								
8								
9								
10								
11								
12								
13								
14								
15								
16								
17								
18								
19								
20								
21								
22								
23								
24								
25								
26								
27								
28								
29								
30								

On this sheet teens note how many hours they volunteered under their name next to the corresponding date. I use this to total their hours at end of their volunteer period.

Are You Between the ages
of 12 and 16?
We want <u>YOU</u> for the Wake
Forest Teen Library Corps

Example of poster displayed in library to recruit TLC volunteers.

October 4-December 10
Applications available
here!
SIGN-UP TODAY!

Summer 2002 Teen Library Corps Volunteers Needed!

Are you are between the ages of 12 and 16?

Would you like to help with projects in and around the library this summer?

Ask us for a Teen Library Corps application.

Fill it out and we will call you to help.

Flexible days and times.

Example of poster displayed in library to recruit TLC volunteers.

Teen Library Corps Application*

Circle one: Fall Winter/Spring Summer

Name:____

Address:____
(include town)

City, State & Zip____________________________________

Phone:____

School:____

Date of Birth: ____________________ Age:________

Interests:____

____

Days and Times Available______________________________

Reference

Name______________________________

Address:______________________________

Phone:______________________________

Teen Signature______________________________

Parent Signature______________________________

*Wake Forest Public Library is looking for new TLC volunteers. We will endeavor to include everyone who volunteers but preference will be given to applicants who have not been part of a prior TLC program.

Copy of application young adults fill out for Teen Library Corps.

PROCEDURES FOR TEEN LIBRARY CORPS VOLUNTEERS

Check in at the Circulation Desk. Note arrival and departure time on the TLC Schedule and total time in TLC notebook on the monthly schedule. You are expected to be prompt. A staff member will inform and direct you in your daily assignments. If the staff are busy when you come in, please begin with your assigned book area.

The staff room will be accessible to TLC members. Personal items can be stored in the sink cabinet designated for TLC.

DRESS CODE

Each TLC participant will receive a T-shirt to be worn tucked in. If an occasion should arise when you are unable to wear your T-shirt, report to a staff member and a TLC Library Badge will be provided for you. Under no circumstances will you serve in the TLC Program without an identifying T-shirt or TLC Badge.

Mandatory Dress Code

- Jeans are acceptable (no holes please)
- Shirts must be tucked in and neat in appearance
- Shorts are acceptable (knee length and hemmed)
- NO tank tops
- NO hats
- NO walkmans or headphones
- NO cell phones
- NO pagers

RESPONSIBILITIES

Possible tasks:
Shelving Books
Creating Book Display Posters
Data Entry using computer
Mending, processing and making changes to books
Withdrawing weeded books and packing for transportation to LAB
Checking in new magazines
Emptying book drop
Maintaining your assigned book collections
Helping librarians with special projects

REMEMBER: You are here to help the librarians; this is not a time for you to socialize or goof off. Corps members not taking their commitment seriously **will be** asked to leave the corps.

Copy of Teen Library Corps procedures given to teens with application and reviewed during interview process.

GUIDELINES FOR TEEN LIBRARY CORPS MEMBERS

You have been selected to be a Teen Library Corps member for Wake Forest Public Library.

Your success will have an impact on the future of the TLC program and we expect that you will perform your duties in a professional and responsible manner. Following are the guidelines you must adhere to while volunteering in the TLC program at Wake Forest.

Arrive and depart according to your assigned schedule.

If a change in schedule becomes necessary, notify the library staff (554-8498) in a timely manner so that arrangements can be made for your absence. As soon as possible, make arrangements to make up your hours.

You are expected to work a minimum 1-hour shift per day with a maximum 2-hour shift per day. Your total commitment for the fall and winter should be at least 20 hours and for the summer should be at least 30 hours.

Do not bring friends or relatives to the library when you are scheduled to work. If your friends come to the library while you are volunteering, remind them you are working and **cannot talk** with them.

REMEMBER: You are here to help the librarians; this is not a time for you to socialize or goof off. Corps members not taking their commitment seriously **will be** asked to leave the corps.

Maintain a courteous attitude with the public. Answer directional questions if you are able; i.e. where is the copy machine, public phone, etc.? However, refer patrons with informational questions to a library staff member. Following are examples of questions that must be referred to the library staff:

> Do you have dinosaur books?
> Do you have a reading list for my third grader?
> Can you show me how to use the computer?

A telephone is available in the staff room and can be used during an _emergency_.

Copy of Teen Library Corps guidelines given to teens after interview; this form is reviewed during the interview.

INTERVIEW QUESTIONS

Applicant's name _____

Introductions

If you have questions ask any of the following staff members

Christina, Lindsey, Kathy, Jane, and Mary Lynn

Responsibilities

Shelving Books

Creating Book Display Posters

Data Entry using computer

Mending, processing and making changes to books

Withdrawing weeded book and packing for transportation to LAB

Checking in new magazines

Emptying book drop

Helping librarians with special projects

Stress the following two items before, during, or after interview:

Do not bring friends or relatives to the library when you are scheduled to work. If your friends come to the library while you are volunteering, remind them you are working and **cannot talk** with them.

REMEMBER: You are here to help the librarians; this is not a time for you to socialize or goof off. Corps members not taking their commitment seriously **will be** asked to leave the corps.

Questions:

Why are you interested in volunteering at the library?

What jobs would you like to do while you are working in the library (list three choices from above)

1.

2.

3.

Have you every volunteered for any other organization?

How many hours can you work weekly? Will you have trouble getting to and from the library?

What schedule would you like to work? (days and times)

Discuss some activities you have been involved in outside of your schoolwork.

Review Guidelines and Dress Code

Would you like to learn to make book displays?
We will have a workshop on
Friday evening, February 8 at 6 p.m.
or
Saturday afternoon, February 9 at 2 p.m.
The workshop should last about 1 1/2 hours.
Please indicate below if you can or cannot attend and the
day that is best for you.

NAME   (Circle appropriate choices)

NAME   YES   NO   Feb. 8   Feb. 9

NAME   YES   NO   Feb. 8   Feb. 9

NAME   YES   NO   Feb. 8   Feb. 9

NAME   YES   NO   Feb. 8   Feb. 9

Copy of sign-up sheet placed in Teen Library Corps notebook.

Display Workshop
Friday, June 28 - 6 p.m.

Please place a check in the appropriate column. (YES if you can come, NO if you cannot come)

	YES	NO
Name		
Name		
Name		
Name		
Name		
Name		
Name		
Name		
Name		
Name		
Name		

This is your chance to learn how to make displays for the library. You will make one at this workshop and it will be used for future book displays.

Copy of sign-up sheet placed in Teen Library Corps notebook.

Friends Book Sale

We Need YOU! May 11

The Friends of Wake Forest Public Library need your help for a couple of hours on Saturday morning, May 11, at 7:30 or 8. The Friends group makes it possible for Wake Forest to have a year round TLC by purchasing shirts and providing funds for an end of year Pizza/Collage party. They would appreciate your help at their annual book sale. The funds raised from this sale allow us to have a TLC program. Please note below if you can or cannot help. Thanks—Jane

	YES	NO
NAME		
NAME		
NAME		
NAME		
NAME		
NAME		
NAME		

Copy of sign-up sheet placed in Teen Library Corps notebook.

Teen Puppeteers

Waco-McLennan County Library, Waco, Texas
www.waco-texas.com/city_depts/libraryservices/libraryservices.htm
Coordinator: Stacy Schimschat, Youth Services Librarian

The Summer Teen Volunteer Program is geared for youth from the ages of thirteen to seventeen, both boys and girls. Recruitment begins in April and May. The librarian sends information to the local paper, hangs posters in the library, mails flyers to area schools, includes the information in the Free Summer Activities Calendar from the Youth Services Department of the library, and submits the information for the Waco-McLennan County Library's website. Teens call the library and are scheduled for an interview. Stacy Schimschat chooses fifteen teens to be part of the teen volunteer club. The requirements are that the teens must attend all meetings and all performances. They meet every Tuesday afternoon throughout June and July from 2:00 to 3:30. During these times, they create a puppet show and play to be presented at the Summer Teen Performances, which are held at all four Waco Library locations. The Teen Puppeteers performed for 882 people in 2002.

During 2002, the Summer Teen Performances were in alliance with the Summer Reading Club theme, Read Across Texas. The teens recorded and performed the puppet show "The Cowboy Who Cried Coyote," which came from the 2002 Texas Reading Club Manual, and they performed a play based on Laurie Lazzaro Knowlton's picture book, *Why Cowboys Sleep With Their Boots On* (Pelican, 1995). Not only do the teens prepare for the summer performance, they also volunteer at the Waco-McLennan County Library booth at three functions: 4th on the Brazos Celebration, Kidzoobilee, and Kids Health Fair. At the booth, the teens lead a spin art activity, a craft project that participants of all ages enjoy. After the craft is made, the teens attach a Waco-McLennan County Library flyer to the art project. Teen volunteers work with their community and promote the library at these events.

STACY'S TIPS: WORKING WITH TEEN VOLUNTEERS

- Teens become very hyper after consuming caffeine or sugar. Don't plan to do much with them after giving them soft drinks, cookies, or candy! At first, I centered our breaks in the middle of our time together. After realizing how wild they got from eating or drinking, I started giving breaks as close to the end of our time together as possible. Breaks are very important; I would not skip a break because this time allows teens to get to know one another.

- The teens volunteering at the libraries are wonderful because they want to be there. One requirement I have when accepting teens is that they are not forced to volunteer—they want to do it. Also, it goes the other way. I make sure that the parent is in correspondence with the teen, also wanting him or her to volunteer for the library.

- I find that teens have many talents. In our beginning sessions as a group, I always ask: Who is my singer? Who is my painter? Who is my designer? Who is my actor? I always find that I get a great mixture of people with different talents.

- Although teens are very responsible, they are also very forgetful. It is very important to keep reminding them of what they need to do. During one session, I told three teens one thing each to bring the following Tuesday. When Tuesday came around, I asked them if they had brought what I asked. Each one said, "Oh! I forgot!" So I call to remind them either the day before they come, or even the same day. When I remind them, they almost always remember.

- Teens love T-shirts. Each year I design a new T-shirt for the teens to wear to our meetings and functions, based on the summer reading club theme. I use artwork from the Texas Reading Club Manual. This year, I chose the armadillo reading a book on his back. At the top, the T-shirt says "2002 Teen Volunteer." Getting a T-shirt makes the volunteers feel very special, part of a club. They wear their shirts proudly, saying, "Oh, I am sorry my T-shirt is a little dirty because I wore it this weekend." A volunteer who came in not wearing her T-shirt she said she woke up and her brother was wearing it!

Teen Volunteer Information

The Youth Services Department of the Waco-McLennan County Library is asking for teen volunteer help. The teen volunteers will meet as a group on Tuesdays from 2:00 p.m. – 3:30 p.m. beginning June 4 – July 30. Teen volunteers must be thirteen years of age to seventeen years old. The group size will be approximately 12 to 15 teens.

The teens will meet on Tuesdays to prepare for a Summer Performance that will be held on July 23, July 24, July 25, and July 26. On Tuesdays, the teens will create a puppet show and organize, as well as practice, a play to be presented at the Summer Performances.

We would like the teens to also volunteer at some of the following library functions that are held throughout the community:

Kid Zoobilee at the Cameron Park Zoo on Saturday, June 29 from 5:00 p.m. to 8:00 p.m.
>   Teens will perform a puppet show and lead in a spin art activity.

Harry Potter Festival at the Central Library on Tuesday, July 30 at 4:00 p.m.
>   Monitor and assist with games, crafts, and more.

4th on the Brazos Celebration located downtown by the Marriott Courtyard Hotel on Thursday, July 4 from 3 p.m. to 10 p.m.
>   Teens will lead in a Spin Art activity.
>   Teens can sign up for a 2 - 4 hour interval.

2nd Annual Battle of the Books Competition at the Central Library on Saturday, August 3 at 3:00 p.m.
>   Teens will monitor competition and record points.

"Hurray For Health" **Kids Health Fair** at the Waco Convention Center on Saturday, August 10 from 10 a.m. to 3 p.m.
>   Teens will lead in a Spin Art activity.

These activities and the Summer Performance will be facilitated by Stacy Schimschat. If interested in using and developing your talents, creativity, and skills for the library, please contact Stacy Schimschat for an interview at 750-5956. I will be happy to hear from you!

TEEN VOLUNTEERS

Fairfax County Public Library, Fairfax, Virginia
www.fairfaxcounty.gov/living/libraries/default.htm
Coordinator: Katharine Wanderer, Volunteer Coordinator

The Fairfax County Public Library consists of eight regional branches, twelve community branches, and the Access Services branch. It has nearly three million books, periodicals, and other items. More than five million visits to one of their library branches are recorded each year, and the library has 490 full-time equivalent employees, including 131 with master's degrees in library science. More than 3,000 volunteers donated 157,985 hours in 2002. In summary, the Fairfax County Public Library is big, and its teen volunteer program reflects its size.

Teens who want to volunteer have several options. Most choose to work as a Regular Student Volunteer or a Summer Student Volunteer. However, depending on their age, teens have several other choices: Adopt-a-Shelf, Grounds Volunteer, Homework Center Tutor, Page Volunteer, and Tech Time for Youth Student Volunteer. Many adult volunteer positions also accept older teens or college students who are still teens. The minimum age for volunteering is twelve, but younger students may participate in family volunteer projects with a parent or other adult supervising.

Teen volunteers work in every part of the library. At Access Services they rewind and clean tapes, shelve, sort carts, keep bookshelves in order, and help inventory the collection. At Administration they photocopy, file, label, stuff envelopes, collate, and distribute to branches. They help the Graphics Department prepare displays, they repair media for the Media Coordinator, they help students in the Homework Center, they assist patrons on the computer terminals, and they even work outside to keep the grounds looking good. Out of the 157,000 volunteer hours contributed at the Fairfax County Public Library in 2002, students contributed 32,000. It's obvious that this library system welcomes and values teenagers!

Student volunteers undergo an informal interview process in order to obtain a position. Most of the branches provide group orientation and training for student volunteers, either at the beginning of an academic quarter, or in June for Summer Reading Program volunteers. A typical orientation would involve a short tour of the branch, including the sign-in desk, kitchen, restrooms, coat closet, work area, public area, etc. The volunteers are introduced to key staff, and given an explanation of the role of the library in the community. They are instructed about the

---

FAIRFAX COUNTY PUBLIC LIBRARY VOLUNTEER POSITION DESCRIPTIONS

- **Position Title:** Student Volunteer (Regular)
- **Branch:** Available at most branches
- **Department:** Children's Department
- **Supervisor:** Children's staff
- **Length of Commitment:** Varies from branch to branch
- **Time Involvement:** Two hours a week
- **Position Summary:** Assists the Children's Services Staff with a variety of clerical tasks and program preparation.
- **Major Responsibilities:** Shelves picture books, paperbacks, and board books. Stamps "date due" cards. Straightens children's area. Prepares craft materials, flannelboards, and posters for programs. Other related tasks.
- **Qualifications:** Ages twelve to eighteen. Dependable.

- **Position Title:** Student Volunteer (Summer)
- **Branch:** Available at most branches
- **Department:** Children's Department
- **Supervisor:** Children's staff
- **Length of Commitment:** Summer (possible extension into school year)
- **Time Involvement:** Two hours per week (minimum)
- **Position Summary:** Assists the Children's Services Staff with preparation for children's programs, assists children with registration for the Summer Reading Program.
- **Major Responsibilities:** Registers children for the Summer Reading Program. Prepares for various story times by cutting out name tags, prepares for various crafts, finger plays, flannelboards, and posters. Stamps date due cards. Shelves paperbacks and picture books. Other related duties.
- **Qualifications:** Students, ages twelve to eighteen.

- **Position Title:** Adopt-A-Shelf Volunteer
- **Branch:** Available at many branches
- **Department:** Circulation
- **Length of Commitment:** Six months (minimum)
- **Time Involvement:** Flexible
- **Position Summary:** Maintains order, accessibility, and appearance of assigned section of shelving.
- **Major Responsibilities:** Identifies books belonging to other branches, returning them to Circulation desk for rerouting. Pulls books with date due card in pocket and brings them to Circulation desk to be checked in. Identifies books requiring mending and places them in mending area with note attached. Reads spine labels and reshelves books that are not in proper order. Shifts books as necessary to assure easy access. Removes all bookmarks, paper, and litter from books and shelves.
- **Qualifications:** Willingness to volunteer. Knowledge of alpha/numeric order.

- **Position Title:** Grounds Volunteer
- **Branch:** Available at most branches
- **Supervisor:** Staff
- **Length of Commitment:** Seasonal
- **Time Involvement:** Two hours per week
- **Position Summary:** Responsible for tidying the landscaped areas around the building.
- **Major Responsibilities:** Pulls weeds, waters plants, rakes, sweeps sidewalks, picks up trash, as needed.
- **Qualifications:** Able to follow directions and work independently. Physical ability as described above. Some knowledge of plants desirable.

program that they'll be helping with (Summer Reading Program, Children's Department services, etc.), their schedule, the importance of being reliable, calling their supervisor when not able to come in, appropriate dress, etc. Training, which could be as a group or one-on-one, would be on the specific tasks associated with their job. Examples of tasks are: registering children for the Summer Reading Program, preparing a craft for a children's program, stamping cards, sorting carts into shelf order, performing simple troubleshooting at Internet stations, signing people up to use the Internet and monitoring the sign-ups, and reading aloud to younger children.

Branch recognition events are typically simple and short (one hour or so), held at the end of a school year for school year volunteers or in August for summer volunteers. There might be an after-school ice cream social or Saturday pizza party, with music, photos of the students, and tokens of appreciation such as pins, buttons, and certificates of recognition. Staff who supervise the students talk informally about each student's contribution. Some branches have tried including youth volunteers in the adult volunteer recognition event, usually lunch or tea. This experience can be mutually informative and rewarding for adults, youth, and the staff, but it has some drawbacks. Some students are uncomfortable attending a lengthy event, and it might be hard to find a time when both groups are available. There can also be a space problem if the event is in the branch meeting room, which is usually the most convenient place to have it.

Occasionally a student is nominated for a Star Volunteer Award for Exceptional Service. Star Volunteers are recognized by the Library Board of Trustees at a dinner and ceremony in April. Student Volunteer Coordinators look for other ways to recognize youth volunteers for outstanding service as well. Nominating a student for a President's Student Service Award (www.student-service-awards.org/awards_with_ss.htm) is one example of a national award that recognizes volunteers depending on their ages and hours of service.

The children's department staff usually supervises the younger students (ages twelve to fifteen). They assist with program preparation, organize picture books, and do other projects for the branch during the school year. In summer, the students staff the registration table for the Summer Reading Program, and they help with summer programs.

The library partners with schools and parents to provide service-learning opportunities for youth. In order to provide successful volunteer experiences, staff structure their program with orientations, training, and detailed time commitments from the teens. It takes a lot of time to train and supervise the teens, but there is more to the program than the labor involved. As Katherine Wanderer states, "This is our opportunity to educate youth about the services of the library and its value to the community. We are growing adult patrons who are enthusiastic library users and ambassadors for the library. Over the years, we see youth volunteers come back as adult volunteers, apply for our jobs, become Friends of the Library, and support us in many other ways. It's not just a student volunteer program, it's also a program for students—a program that provides enrichment to our teen population in the same way as a book discussion or a video workshop does." Clearly, the Fairfax County Public Library values and supports the needs of teens in the community, and provides the resources to support a quality teen volunteer program.

- **Position Title:** Homework Center Tutor
- **Branch:** Several
- **Department:** Information
- **Supervisor:** Information Staff
- **Length of Commitment:** School year
- **Time Involvement:** Two hours per week
- **Position Summary:** Assists elementary and intermediate school students with their homework assignments.
- **Major Responsibilities:** Welcomes students to the Homework Center. Helps students understand and organize their homework assignment. Guides students in completing assignments. With the staff, assists the student in learning how to use the library for a homework assignment. Encourages and supports the efforts of students to complete homework in a timely and accurate fashion.
- **Qualifications:** Experience with children. Teaching/training and library skills. Good interpersonal skills. Patience. Must be available during after school hours or on Saturday.

- **Position Title:** Page Volunteer
- **Branch:** Available at most branches
- **Department:** Page Department
- **Supervisor:** Page Supervisor
- **Length of Commitment:** Six months to a year
- **Time Involvement:** Three hours per week (minimum)
- **Position Summary:** Responsible for accurately shelving several library formats and subject areas of the library, plus performing general support work in the Page Department.

- **Major Responsibilities:** Stamps daily date due cards for books and videos; puts carts in order; shelves paperbacks, edges and dusts shelves, may shelf read and/or shelve carts (particularly JP's, JR's and FIC). Sets up meeting room and other duties as assigned. May do photocopier or computer assignments.
- **Qualifications:** Must be fourteen years of age or older. Must follow direction well. Ability to concentrate and pay attention to details. Ability to lift books and push book carts; bending required. Must be able to work independently after being instructed.

- **Position Title:** Tech Time for Youth Student Volunteer
- **Location:** Sherwood Regional Library
- **Supervisor:** Children's Librarian
- **Length of Commitment:** At least six months
- **Time Involvement:** Two hours per week, Mondays or Thursdays: 4:00 to 6:00 p.m. Lab may be open additional hours in the future.
- **Position Summary:** Helps students use electronic equipment and resources in the Sherwood Tech Training Lab.
- **Major Responsibilities:** After completing our training program, assists students with Internet search strategies and keyboarding techniques using Microsoft Word.
- **Qualifications:** Ages sixteen to eighteen. Enjoys helping people. Familiar with Internet and has basic word processing skills.

RECOGNIZING EXCELLENT VOLUNTEER SERVICE

How do you reward volunteer service that is so exemplary that it deserves something special? You promote the volunteer! One of the volunteers at the Salina Public Library, Travis Haugh, started volunteering when he was in sixth grade, even without applying. When he discovered that he missed the deadline, he just showed up at the children's room and started helping out so much that the staff let him officially volunteer without going through the formal process. His initiative has not waned. Now a junior in high school, he has volunteered at the library every summer and has recently been promoted to teen volunteer coordinator, at his request. As coordinator, he has interviewed dozens of teens for prospective volunteer positions; scheduled their shifts around vacation, job, and summer school plans; and developed a computer program to keep track of statistics. And he's gaining valuable experience that is sure to help him in his future career in business management. (See the photograph of Travis Haugh on the cover of *VOYA*'s April 2002 issue, reprinted on the next page.)

Teen Volunteer Program

Salina Public Library, Salina, Kansas
www.salpublib.org
Coordinator: Kristi L. Hanson, Youth Services Coordinator

The Teen Volunteer Program was started almost nine years ago and has grown every year since then. In 2001 there were nearly seventy teen volunteers, ages twelve to seventeen. The program runs during the summer, and the volunteers' main responsibility is to register children for the Summer Reading Program. Since there are more than 2,000 children who sign up each summer, this job takes most of their time. However, they also coordinate the weekly games, empty the book drop, straighten shelves, help with programs, and assist with the summer reading program party for about 800 people. The teen volunteers worked a total of 2,210 hours during the summer of 2001.

Recruitment is done in the spring. Applications are taken to the schools and are available in the library and on the website. Interested students complete and return the application by the deadline and are called for an interview. The interview is good experience for the teen; it also reinforces the serious nature of the job. During the interview, the staff explains the job and responsibilities, asks questions to learn more about the potential volunteer, and goes over a contract explaining the volunteering rules, which is signed by both the teen and his or her parent or guardian.

As part of the training process, the teens are encouraged to attend a three-hour session called "The In-Credible Teen Workshop," which features a motivational speaker. The volunteers learn skills that will help them in their personal lives as well as in their library volunteer work. Lunch is provided; the workshop serves as a social occasion and the volunteers can talk and visit with one another.

The Summer Reading Program Party could not happen without the teen volunteers. It is held outside the library on a Friday evening from 6:00 to 8:00. This party is a reward for all the children who have reached their goals during the summer reading program. Up to 800 people have attended this event. The teens help prepare for the party by making cotton candy, bagging popcorn, cooking hot dogs, and setting up tables and chairs before everyone arrives. Several volunteers help paint faces and run the fishpond during the party. They also help with prize drawings at the end of the party.

The teen volunteers receive a T-shirt to wear while working at the library, purchased by the Friends of the Salina Public Library. In addition, they are rewarded with a Teen Volunteer Appreciation night at the end of the summer. The teens are invited to bring two guests, and each volunteer is awarded with a certificate of appreciation containing the number of hours worked that summer. In addition, the Friends of the Library is in the process of establishing a Teen Volunteer Scholarship for teens who have volunteered at the Salina Public Library. The criteria for eligibility is still being determined.

The library magazine serving those who serve young adults

Voice of Youth Advocates

VOL. 25
No. 1

APRIL

2002

- Best Science Fiction, Fantasy, and Horror 2001

- Fantasy for People Who Don't Like Fantasy

- Showing Anime in the Library

- A Bad Case of the Internet Ethics Blues

Interview Details and Questions--Summer Teen Volunteer

1. Give details of the volunteer experience: This is what the job entails
   - --registering participants
   - --conducting games and contests
   - --straightening shelves
   - --getting bookdrop
   - --other special projects, such as helping with programs, getting crafts ready, etc.

2. What things do you think are important for volunteers to do? (Give interviewee a chance to answer this question; then tell the prospective volunteer how important the tasks below are.) **It's very important that you:**

--Be on time for shift and not to leave early without permission.

--Call in ahead of time if you are sick and cannot work your shift. We really depend on our volunteers and would need to try to cover your shift.

--Dress appropriately. No cut-offs or really short skirts. Jeans and shorts are fine. We do expect you to wear the really cool T-shirt we give you. It makes it easier for everyone to identify you as a teen volunteer, including the staff upstairs.

--Treat everyone with respect and courtesy, not only the patrons, but the staff and other volunteers.

--Follow library rules. That means:
   - --No swearing or hurtful language.
   - --No graffiti in or outside the library.
   - --**Absolutely NO ALCOHOL OR DRUGS**.

--Cooperate with other volunteers and library staff.

--Share volunteer responsibilities with other volunteers. Do your part, but allow the other volunteers the chance to do theirs.

--You can't bring younger brothers and sisters, friends, or children for whom you are baby-sitting to work with you. It's not fair to them and you can't concentrate on your job.

-- What if you're working your shift and some of your friends come in and want to sit and chat? How would you handle the situation?

-- Being a teen volunteer is an important part of our SRP. You should be proud of the work you do and act accordingly.

3. Can you tell me about something you have done that you're proud of?

4. Would you like to ask me any questions?

5. Knowing what you now know about being a volunteer, would you still like to be one? (If they say yes, explain the contract and have them sign it, let them take it for their parents to sign)

<u>VERY IMPORTANT INFORMATION FOR VOLUNTEERS TO KNOW</u>

<u>When you arrive for your volunteer shift, please sign-in</u> on the volunteer sign-in sheet at the Youth Services Desk and have a Youth Services staff member initial next to your name.

When you are ready to leave from your volunteer shift, <u>please sign-out</u> and have a Youth Services staff member initial next to your name.

If you do not sign-in or sign-out, we may assume that you arrived late for your volunteer shift or that you left early from your volunteer shift without permission.

_____

If people need

- --help finding books or other materials,
- --directions on how to find a book or other material,
- --help using any of the computers,
- --to know other information about the Library
- --to know information about the Summer Reading Program (and the questions/answers aren't listed on the "Summer Reading Program Information Sheet" or on the "Frequently Asked Summer Reading Program Questions" sheet),
- --to sign up for storytime or to get information about storytime,
- --to sign up for other programs or to get information about other programs,

please ask them to come to the Youth Services Checkout Desk, and our non-volunteer staff will help them.

THANK YOU ALL FOR AGREEING TO BE SUMMER TEEN VOLUNTEERS!

SUMMER READING PROGRAM TEEN VOLUNTEER CONTRACT

Congratulations on being accepted as a teen volunteer for the Salina Public Library Summer Teen Volunteer program.

This contract lets you know the responsibilities and the benefits associated with being a volunteer. Your schedule will be mailed to you as soon as the interviews are completed.

If you have any problems with your volunteer schedule, please contact the Youth Services Department immediately at (785) 825-4624.

VOLUNTEERING: WHAT YOU GET

The most important reward that teen volunteers receive is the satisfaction of knowing that they have helped their community and that they have been good role models for other kids.

All teen volunteers also receive a "Teen Volunteer" T-shirt that they should wear when they come to volunteer at the library.

Teen volunteers who successfully complete their volunteer schedule and who <u>follow all the terms of this contract</u> will also be invited (along with their parents) to a special "Appreciation Party" at the end of the summer. At the party, teen volunteers will be recognized and receive awards.

VOLUNTEERING: WHAT YOU GIVE

Volunteers Should

1. <u>Be on time for their volunteer shifts and should not leave early from their shift</u> without permission from a Youth Services staff member.

2. <u>Notify the Youth Services Department</u>—(785) 825-4624—at least 2 hours before their volunteer shift is to start if they are sick and/or not able to work.

3. <u>Dress appropriately</u>. Volunteers should wear the volunteer T-shirt with jeans, pants, shorts, or a skirt. Clothes should be clean and should not have any holes, tears, or shreds that can be seen. Clothes should not have any writing or pictures on them of tobacco products, alcohol, or drugs. Volunteers should not wear clothing that covers the volunteer T-shirt. If you have any questions, please talk with a Youth Services staff member.

4. <u>Treat everyone with respect and courtesty at all times</u>.
   --Volunteers should exhibit a helpful attitude to everyone.
   --Volunteers should cooperate with other volunteers and with all library staff.
   --Volunteers should focus on and share volunteer responsibilities with other volunteers.

5. Take pride in the important volunteer work that they do at the library and act accordingly.
    --Volunteers should follow all library rules for appropriate behavior in the library.
        (Please do not yell or shout. Please do not run or wrestle.)
    --Volunteers should respect library property by not marking on library furniture or on library materials.
    --Volunteers should leave the volunteer area in a clean and neat manner.
    --Volunteers should not swear or use hurtful language.
    --When volunteers are working, they should keep conversations with friends short, so as not to interfere with their volunteer responsibilities. Volunteers are welcome to stay at the library and visit with friends before or after their volunteer shifts.

Volunteers Should Not

1. Bring younger brothers or sisters, friends, or children for which they are baby-sitting to work with them. Please do not agree to baby-sit during the times that you are scheduled to volunteer, or if you have to baby-sit, please call the Youth Services Department—(785) 825-4624—to reschedule your shift.

2. Bring valuable personal items to the library. Volunteers do not have any place to store valuable items. The library is a public place, and library staff cannot be responsible for any lost or stolen items.

If you have any questions about the volunteer program, please come talk with a Youth Services Department staff member. We want your volunteer experience to be enjoyable for you as well as for the people you are helping.

If any volunteer does not follow the terms of this contract, the Youth Services Department reserves the right to dismiss that volunteer from the volunteer program. Should such a situation arise, the volunteer will be notified and all future volunteer time will be cancelled.

Any volunteer who brings any tobacco products, alcohol, or drugs to the library (even if that person is not volunteering at that time) will be dismissed immediately.

X _____   Date _____
     Kristi L. Hansen
     Youth Services Coordinator

My signature below indicates that I understand and agree to the terms listed in this contract.

X _____   Date _____

X _____   Date _____
     Parent or Legal Guardian's Signature

Reach Out and Read (R.O.A.R.) Corps

Winchester Public Library, Winchester, Massachusetts
www.winpublib.org
Staff Contact: Yvonne K. Coleman, Head of Children's Services

R.O.A.R. is a teen library volunteer program designed to bring books and reading to preschool- and elementary-age children. Teens aged eleven to seventeen travel around to different places in the community—some scheduled for an audience and some not—and read to children wherever they are. They read to groups, small and large, at the playgrounds, the pond beach, the Swim Club, the Boat Club, the Recreation Department Camp, the program for special-needs children, the local drama school, the grocery store, the bagel shop, toy stores, the bookstore, and of course, the bank. If they have no scheduled stops, they look for children in casual settings and read to just a few. One mother, overheard in the library, was applauding the work of the Corps. "One day I was in line at the Post Office. The kids were getting restless, but the R.O.A.R. Corps was there and read to them. It was great!" One member, Alice Kronenberg, summed it up by saying "R.O.A.R. was a really exciting experience for me. I interacted with kids while they learned how much fun reading was. The best thing was seeing the kids ask questions about the story. That showed they were really listening."

The Winchester Public Library, part of the Minuteman Library Network, serves a community of 20,000 people, eight miles north of Boston. The town is among the highest in the area in terms of income per capita, and a recent poll named the library as the most respected service in the town. An influx of very young children in recent years has created a need for educational play experiences. R.O.A.R. readers thus help to fulfill that need for cultural stimulation for the young. Ongoing for ten years, this outreach program is cosponsored by the Winchester Cooperative Bank and the Winchester Public Library. Each spring the library youth services staff makes a proposal to the bank to fund the R.O.A.R. Corps Coordinator, and supporting materials such as T-shirts, film for photos, mileage, special car insurance, and other items. Although this proposal funds other components of the summer program for adults as well, it is the R.O.A.R. Corps of teen volunteers that has been the biggest success. This past summer showed an increase in the number of volunteers, from a typical twenty or twenty-five to more than forty.

Volunteers must be entering seventh grade in order to participate, so there is always a fresh group of new teens combined with the experienced readers. So far, no selection process has been needed, as all volunteers who apply have been accommodated. Some love volunteering so much that they complete more than the required hours. There is an early training session at the outset of the summer, and ongoing training each morning as they choose the books that they would like to read that day. The teens are shown how to read picture books and encouraged to select books that they personally enjoy. The Children's Department has purchased a group of favorites, the R.O.A.R. Collection, so that they are always available. Many teens have personal favorites. "We read some of the books so many times that we could recite them from memory," said Corps member Kara Foley.

The library was recently invited to honor Corps members at a town youth service banquet. The youth services staff chose several volunteers who had been involved for more than two years. Time given is the only real criteria, as all volunteers have equal merit. Each volunteer also receives a formal letter that can be included with college applications. They are proud to be associated with R.O.A.R. Some have even been known to wear the black T-shirt with the lion logo to school!

The key to this program's success is the coordinator, and the staff considers themselves lucky in that regard. The program coordinator needs to be a mature adult who has the ability to relate to both teens and young children, has a love of and knowledge of children's books, and can serve as a model for reading those books. Also, some of the reading sites must be "trained" in what to expect from the readers. For example, the camp supervisors need to stay with the groups to monitor behavior, and the site must adhere to time schedules as well, since their days are busy ones. In other words, the Corps must always exude a professional demeanor. Any problems that have occurred have been from the reading sites. Sometimes they have not been prepared for the teen volunteers or have not realized the professional nature of the service. The Corps members have always been outstanding young people, and the library staff demands that they be treated with the respect that is due them.

Dennis Kronenberg, a teacher at the middle school, has been the R.O.A.R. Coordinator for the past four years. He is Mr. R.O.A.R. to the staff, the teens, and the community. He testifies to the program's success: "Some of the impressions that stay with me are the moments when my readers really connect with children. It happens so often. You can see the children enjoying a great story, but you can also see the child still alive in the reader. Their sharing is honest and meaningful to them. They have not lost their inner child and they enjoy the moment just as much. It makes the experience special for both. I am proud of the way they represent the library and the Winchester Cooperative Bank. The community can see these fine examples of our future."

The benefits of this program are many. Not only do the teens learn about working with children, they learn about their community. Furthermore, the volunteers reach many people who have never visited the library or don't know about the many programs and services available there. Says Yvonne Coleman, Head of Children's Services, "When I hatched the idea for the R.O.A.R. Corps, I truly had no idea that it would become such a huge success. Yet I inherently knew that the experience would be beneficial to both readers and listeners. Not all of the Corps members are naturally outgoing. Each brings his or her own special personality to the experience, and each is ultimately changed by it." Their efforts have proven to be successful for the teens, who learn the power of story; the library, which grows beyond its walls; and the children, who discover a love for reading and books.

SELECTED BIBLIOGRAPHY

America's Children 2002. www.childstats.gov (15 Aug. 2002).

Bard, Therese Bissen. *Student Assistants in the School Library Media Center.* Englewood, Colo.: Libraries Unlimited, 1999.

Bartlett, Linda. "Intergenerational Internet." *Voice of Youth Advocates* 24 (October 2001): 259.

Coleman, Yvonne. "Teen Corps Reaches Out With Pride." *Journal of Youth Services in Libraries* 9 (Spring 1996): 243–47.

Cooper, Mark. "Big Dummy's Guide to Service-Learning." Florida International University. www.fiu.edu/~time4chg/Library/bigdummy.html (12 Aug. 2002).

Driggers, Preston F. "Risk Management for Volunteer Programs." *Colorado Libraries* 26 (Fall 2000): 40–41.

Driggers, Preston, and Eileen Dumas. *Managing Library Volunteers: A Practical Toolkit.* Chicago: ALA Editions, 2002.

Eisenhut, Lynn. "Teen Volunteers." *Voice of Youth Advocates* 11 (June 1988): 65–70.

"Facts for Families." American Academy of Child and Adolescent Psychiatry. 1997. www.aacap.org/publications/factsfam/develop.htm (27 July 2002).

Farmer, Lesley S. J. *Training Student Library Staff.* Worthington, Ohio: Linworth Publishing, Inc., 1997.

Lynch, Rick. "Seven Deadly Sins of Supervisors." *CASA Resources.* 1993. www.casanet.org/programs-management/personnel/sins.htm (12 Aug. 2002).

McCune, Bonnie. "Marketing to Find Volunteers." *Colorado Libraries* 26 (Fall 2000): 40–41.

_____. "The New Volunteerism: Making It Pay Off for Your Library." *American Libraries* 24, no. 9 (October 93): 822–25.

McCune, Bonnie, and Charlezine "Terry" Nelson. *Recruiting and Managing Volunteers in Libraries: A How To Do It Manual.* New York: Neal-Schuman Publishers, 1995.

McCurley, Steve. "How to Fire a Volunteer and Live to Tell About It." *CASA Resources.* 1993. www.casanet.org/program-management/volunteer-manage/fire.htm (12 Aug. 2002).

McCurley, Steve, and Rick Lynch. *Essential Volunteer Management.* Downers Grove, Ill.: Heritage Arts, 1989.

McGrath, Marsha, and Jana R. Fine. "Teen Volunteers in the Library." *Public Libraries* 29 (January/February 1990): 24–28.

Sager, Don. "Beyond Volunteerism: Community Service Programs and Public Libraries." *Public Libraries* (May/June 1999): 149–53.

Schondel, Connie K., and Kathryn E. Boehm. "Motivational Needs of Adolescent Volunteers." *Adolescence* 35, no. 138 (Summer 2000): 335–44.

Smallwood, Carol. "Training Students and Adult Assistants, Interns, and Volunteers." *Book Report* 17 (January/February 1999): 24–26.

"2001–2002 State of Our Nation's Youth." Horatio Alger Association of Distinguished Americans, 2002. www.horatioalger.com/pubmat/submit01.cfm (10 Aug. 2002).

Wilson, Marlene. *Effective Management of Volunteer Programs.* Boulder, Colo.: Volunteer Management Associates, 1976.

Zinser, Jana. "Mandating Community Service: Service or Servitude?" *State Legislatures* 19, no. 3 (March 1993): 30–33.

FURTHER READING

Baldwin, Liz. "It All Started in the Summer . . ." *Journal of Youth Services in Libraries* 9 (Spring 1996): 250–52.

Instructions on starting a summer teen volunteer program.

Farmer, Lesley S. J. "Managing Volunteers Through Managing Yourself." *Book Report* 13, no. 4 (January/February 1995): 19–21.

Explains that a successful volunteer program is based on quality management from the volunteer coordinator.

Foster, Jackie, and Rosemary Knapp. "Tips and Other Bright Ideas." *Book Report* 11, no. 3 (November/December 1992): 8–12.

A list of tips relating to students and parents who volunteer in a school library.

Morris, Jacqueline G. "School Media Specialists Plan for Successful Volunteer Programs." *Indiana Media Journal* 3 (1980): 7–8.

Successful programs start with a five-step plan to expand library services and instruction by using volunteers in the school library.

"Online Resources for Volunteer Managers and Service Leaders." Virtual Volunteering Project. 2000. www.serviceleader.org/vv/vonline.html (12 Aug. 2002).

Comprehensive index to resources for every aspect of volunteer management, recruitment, recognition, evaluation, risk management, and promotion.

"Teens: The Community Service Solution." Public Library Community Service Project. 2000. www.colapublib.org/teen (10 Sept. 2002).

Practical information on developing a teen community service program based on five models.

YALSA Professional Development Center. 2002. www.ala.org/yalsa/profdev/programming.html (12 July 2002).

Contains lots of resources for teen volunteering, including web links, articles, books, and other documents.

Youth Service America. 2002. www.ysa.org (12 July 2002).

Includes templates, awards, articles, events, and an interactive planning tool to support service projects.

Appendix A

Top Ten Myths and Realities of Working with Teen Volunteers

KELLIE SHOEMAKER

Over the last fifteen years, the Mesa Public Library in Mesa, Arizona, has developed an extensive teen volunteer program. Not only do we have the Young Adult Advisory Council and a volunteer group that produces our literary magazine called **FRANK**, we use fifteen volunteers during the school year and thirty volunteers during the summer in our Young Adult Room. These volunteers commit to working a two- or three-hour weekly shift, and they perform a variety of tasks which include covering paperbacks with laminate, registering participants and distributing prizes for our summer reading program, preparing materials for storytimes, folding brochures, and a myriad of other things.

I am not an expert on teen volunteers. I just pretend to be one in my position as volunteer supervisor for young adults at the library. But after working with teens for six years in various volunteer situations, I have learned a great deal about the expectations, behaviors, policies, and attitudes that can affect a volunteer program and determine its success or failure. After thinking through all the mistakes I've made and wishing someone older and wiser and warned me about them, I compiled the following helpful hints, which I call the Top Ten Myths and Realities of Teen Volunteers.

MYTH #10: Kids who hang around the library a lot will make good volunteers.

REALITY: Actually, this might be true some of the time, especially for some volunteer jobs like teen advisory councils. But often teenagers who hang around the library are only there because they have nowhere else to go. They may not like books, helping people, or even helping you. Watch them and their behavior awhile before you ask them to commit to a regular volunteer position.

MYTH #9: If a teen goes to the trouble of filling out an application, he or she really wants to volunteer.

REALITY: The first summer of my first professional position, I set up my first young adult volunteer program called "Ready Readers." The premise was simple: teens signed up, attended a training session, and came to the library at designated times to read to preschool children. During the training session, one of the boys

Young Adult Volunteer Andy Canada giving game to patron.

did not participate at all. He did not practice reading to a partner, he did not look through the selected picture books, and he did not look at me. He obviously did not want to be there. Afterwards I asked he if he wanted to do this, and he told me no. Why did he sign up? He said, "My mother made me."

My first mistake when working with teen volunteers was not screening and interviewing them. If I had asked the right questions, I could have saved all of us time and aggravation. Ask prospective volunteers why they want to volunteer, how long they can commit, and whether they can get transportation. Ask them what they enjoy doing and tell them about the tasks they will be asked to complete. Be honest. Are there slow periods with nothing to do? Repetitive tasks? Tell them. Find out if each volunteer can work alone and be self-motivated. And if he or she does not seem interested, don't take the candidate, or you'll be setting up both your program and your volunteer for failure.

MYTH #8: Parents aren't important to the teen's involvement in a volunteer program.

REALITY: I know this one is rather obvious at first, but often we don't think about the parents when we are talking to a prospective volunteer. First of all, the parent must come with the teen to the interview. It shows a willingness on the parent's part to support the teen's commitment, and the interview is a good time to talk about issues like transportation, schedules, substitutes, policies, training, dependability, and responsibilities at home and school. The parent has to help teach the young adult what life in the working world is like: we call in when we are sick, we have to give up social activities if conflicts arise, we have to make other arrangements if the car breaks down, and so on. The volunteer supervisor and the parent work together as a team to teach the young adult the skills that will make him or her successful in a first working experience, even one without pay.

MYTH #7: It's easy to incorporate young adult volunteers into your work schedule.

REALITY: No matter how much you try, how dedicated you are to your job, or how much you want your volunteer program to succeed, you need the support and commitment of the people who work with you. You cannot be at the library every hour it is

Mesa Public Library
Young Adult Area
Volunteer Application

Date _____

Name _____

Address _____

City _____ Zip _____

Phone _____

Date of Birth _____

School _____

Grade _____

Special hobbies or interests:

_____

_____

_____

Other activities or clubs:

_____

_____

_____

What are your reasons for volunteering?

_____

_____

_____

Volunteering is like having a job. We count on you to be here at a certain time. Volunteers are asked to work at least 2 hours a week.
What times can you work as a volunteer?

Days _____

Times _____

IN EMERGENCY, CONTACT:

Name _____

Home Phone _____

Business Phone _____

Name of Parent or Guardian

_____

Address _____

Phone _____
Signature of Parent or Guardian consenting to applicant's working as a volunteer:

_____

I hereby apply for work as a volunteer in the Young Adult Area of the Mesa Public Library. I understand that if I am accepted, I will be expected to show up and work when I am scheduled. I will notify a librarian in the Young Adult Area if I can't work as scheduled.

_____
Applicant's Signature

_____
Date

DROP BY

Mesa Public Library

*We can use
your help
in our
Young Adult
Volunteer Program*

**Young Adult Room
Mesa Public Library
64 E. 1st Street
644-2734**

open and you cannot be at your supervising post every time a volunteer needs you. So, the first step is to find other staff members who feel comfortable working with teenagers and who are committed to your program's success.

It may be easy to incorporate adult volunteers into your work schedule, but teens are never easy to incorporate anywhere. They need you to give them patience, attention, and encouragement. Be prepared to spend a lot of time interviewing, explaining, showing, chatting, explaining some more, scheduling, record-keeping, calling, and explaining a third time. If you know ahead of time that you will have to juggle your schedule and get help from others, you will be more relaxed and better able to handle the demands that are placed upon you.

MYTH #6: Enthusiasm equals commitment.

REALITY: This maxim may be true for a librarian, but it is not necessarily true for a teenage volunteer. Today it's hot, tomorrow it's not. As my sixteen-year-old daughter frequently tells me, "That's so eighties, Mom!" which implies that anything lasting more than a decade is the worst thing imaginable. Since she was

born in 1981, I like to tell her that she's "so eighties" too, but the irony is lost on her. In fact, I told her I was going to quote her about the eighties, and she said, "Even the nineties make me sick," which further illustrates my point, I think.

This is not to say that volunteer supervisors *don't* look for enthusiasm. Enthusiasm is very important in a prospective volunteer, but it's not the most important quality. Look for other qualities, too, like style, personality, time schedule, and any physical, emotional, or mental limitations. Match the job to the volunteer. Is the position one in which the volunteer deals with the public? You might need someone who is personable and outgoing. Is your candidate involved in extracurricular activities? It may seem odd, but the busier a teenager is, the more committed he or she will probably be, having learned how to manage time. What are the volunteer's values? Find out what your candidate considers to be important and you'll get a good insight into what kind of volunteer you will have for your program.

Young Adult Volunteer Allison Coons covering paperbacks with laminate. Photos by Kellie Shoemaker.

MYTH #5: If a young adult wants to quit a volunteer position, he or she will just tell you.

REALITY: Sometimes you will be told. One girl told me she had some "bad news" and asked to come into my office. After saying, "I don't know how to tell you this," and "please don't be mad at me," she told me what I had already guessed: she was quitting. I don't know if she expected me to have a nervous breakdown or to burst into tears, but I probably disappointed her with my response. I jumped out of the chair where she had wanted me to sit to better handle the shock and said, "Okay, when's your last day?" Maybe it wasn't the most appropriate thing to do (a little dismay would have been better), but I couldn't help it. We volunteeer supervisors have to have fun somehow, don't we?

Actually, what that volunteer did was much preferable to what sometimes happens. Either volunteers are nervous or shy about telling you they want to stop volunteering, or they might not even realize it themselves, so they *show* you they are ready to give it up. Maybe they'll just stop coming in when they are supposed to, or they won't want to do anything you ask them, or they'll leave the desk for long periods to do other things. If I'm experiencing behavior or attendance problems, my first response is to ask them if they still want to volunteer. Often they don't and are quite relieved to say so.

MYTH #4: A teen volunteer will tell you if he or she does not enjoy the job.

REALITY: By not enjoying the job, I don't mean complaining about certain aspects of the position. Teens have no problem letting you know they don't enjoy covering books. I'm referring to the volunteer position itself. I recently discovered that one boy did not like volunteering, yet he had been with us for about a year and a half. He is a very quiet person who always shows up on time, does what we ask and goes home. I don't think I would have found out about his feelings if I had not completed an evaluation of his performance and asked him also to evaluate us. We have since talked about his tasks and I have assigned him some things to do to make his shift more interesting. I hope he will be happier when volunteering and that his next evaluation will be more positive.

We have recently started evaluating our volunteers, and I'm learning a lot of things I would not have known otherwise. Yes, it does take more time and schedule-juggling, but the benefits are many. Evaluations give you a way to let volunteers know how they are doing—both good and bad. They give you documentation if you are ever asked for references, provide you with feedback on your management style, and point out what works or doesn't with the volunteer program itself.

MYTH #3: It's easy to get rid of a volunteer who's not performing to your standards.

REALITY: Well, it used to be easy at the Mesa Public Library. For many years before I started, the supervisor would just tell the volunteer that his or her behavior wasn't appropriate and don't bother to come back, thank you very much. Then I took over as the volunteer supervisor and guess what happened? Vinnie Volunteer, the teenager from hell.

We are lucky at the Mesa Public Library; about two years ago we hired a volunteer coordinator who oversees our volunteer program. I could add another myth to the list and say that hiring a volunteer coordinator will save you time, but right off the bat she made the supervisors do many things we hadn't done before, like write job descriptions, develop policies and procedures, conduct

evaluations, and, believe it or not, attend volunteer managers' meetings! An important aspect of her job is offering orientations to new library volunteers, during which she discusses our policies and expectations. Then she has them sign a work agreement and an attendance policy. I am explaining this process because if our volunteer coordinator had been here when we hired Vinnie, we never would have had a problem firing him.

Vinnie had been driving me crazy for about a year before I pleaded for help. He was rude to patrons, he would disappear for long periods of time, he didn't want to do any work that was given to him, and worst of all, he argued with me and other staff members whenever we corrected him. Our coordinator agreed to call his house and explain the situation to his parents. Unfortunately, his mother did not understand at all. Vinnie would be crushed, she said. He loved his job, she said. How could we do this with no warning?

Warning? We had assumed that our constant nagging at Vinnie *had* served as a kind of warning, but it was true that nothing "official" had been served. Therefore, under threat of hysterical parent, we drafted a document called the "Youth Volunteer Conduct Agreement." When a volunteer's work performance is not satisfactory, and he or she wants to continue working, we now have a "Volunteer Discipline Policy" in which we meet with the volunteer and parent. We discuss the undesirable behavior, explain the consequences of not changing the behavior, and ask them both to sign the conduct agreement. Then the volunteer is considered to be "on probation" and appropriately warned.

As you might imagine, Vinnie is no longer with us. His argumentative nature proved to be his downfall. Since then we have had to utilize the agreement with two other volunteers, but I'm thankful to report that there have been no lawsuits filed as yet. Keep your fingers crossed.

MYTH #2: Teens volunteer because they need something to do.

REALITY: Teenagers today have plenty to do. There are sports teams, both at school and in the community. There are lessons for everything conceivable—music, dance, art, voice, the martial arts, photography, and much more. There are numerous school clubs. There are afterschool jobs for all ages. There are household chores and responsibilities. And there are the fun things: driving around with friends, going to the mall, watching movies and television, talking on the phone, using the computer. And what about homework? Teens have more things to do than ever before. So why do teens want to volunteer?

Work experience. Not only can they cite their volunteer experience, they need you as a a reference, especially important in getting their first job.

Class or club credit. Many schools and organizations require than teens donate time to their community. Sometimes they even need their volunteer hours to pass a course or to earn credit to graduate.

College applications. It's getting harder and harder to get into college these days. As this generation becomes ready for college, it will become even more competitive. Teens know that volunteer experience looks good on an application and might give them the edge they need to get into the school of their choice.

Volunteer opportunities can help teens to develop personal and social skills, including self esteem, giving them a chance to interact socially in another setting. All these benefits motivate teens to volunteer in the library, and we need to be motivated to give them the best experience we can while they're with us.

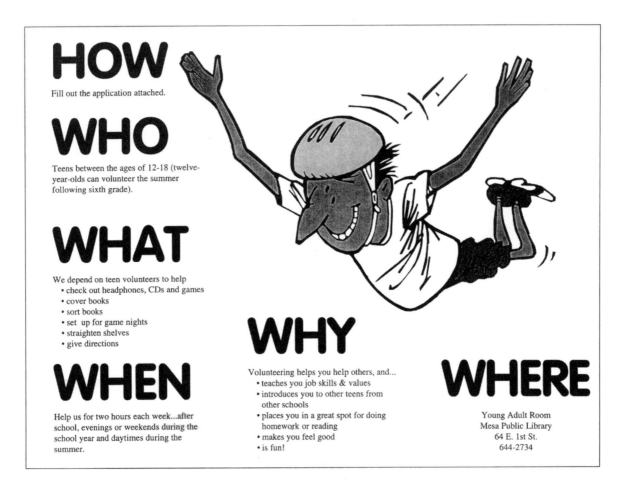

HOW

Fill out the application attached.

WHO

Teens between the ages of 12-18 (twelve-year-olds can volunteer the summer following sixth grade).

WHAT

We depend on teen volunteers to help
- check out headphones, CDs and games
- cover books
- sort books
- set up for game nights
- straighten shelves
- give directions

WHEN

Help us for two hours each week...after school, evenings or weekends during the school year and daytimes during the summer.

WHY

Volunteering helps you help others, and...
- teaches you job skills & values
- introduces you to other teens from other schools
- places you in a great spot for doing homework or reading
- makes you feel good
- is fun!

WHERE

Young Adult Room
Mesa Public Library
64 E. 1st St.
644-2734

Finally, MYTH #1 about teen volunteers: USING TEEN VOLUNTEERS WILL SAVE YOU TIME.

REALITY: This is the biggest misconception in the library world. If you are using or thinking about using teen volunteers to save time, you may want to reconsider having a young adult volunteer program. Using *adult* volunteers will save you loads of time, but there are many other factors to consider when evaluating teen volunteers and time.

I came to a realization that has helped me immensely in my role as a young adult volunteer supervisor:

The mission of a young adult volunteer program is to help and support teens by providing the environment, experience, and training they need to become responsible adults in our community.

In other words, having teen volunteers is like having a summer reading program, or visiting schools, or preparing a bibliography—we do it for our patrons as part of our commitment to serve young adults. It means that we have to spend a good chunk of our work time to make this program successful.

Will volunteers help the library? Of course they will. Not only do they do a multitude of tasks, they become connected to the library and familiar with its resources. Many teens who seldom visited the library before volunteering become regular users, even after their volunteering time is over.

Will volunteers save you time? Adult volunteers definitely will, but teen volunteers need more of your tender loving care. If you did a time-analysis study comparing the number of hours you spend supervising teen volunteers with the number of hours it would take to do the tasks you assign to them, it would be heavier on the supervising side, because some tasks you would do yourself and other tasks simply would not get done.

Whether this piece is titled, "Myths and Realities of Working With Teen Volunteers" or "Mistakes I Made and What I Learned From Them," I hope I have not dissuaded you from using teen volunteers in your library. The success stories far outweigh the unsuccessful ones. Working with teen volunteers can be rewarding and fun, especially as you watch little twelve-year-olds mature into responsible adults ready for college. They are also known to tell good jokes, offer valuable advice, and keep you humble when they catch you making a mistake. Most importantly, a teen volunteer program is a good way of providing an important service to a segment of our population that is desperate for the skills, talents, and abilities that we can help them discover in themselves.

Kellie Shoemaker is a young adult librarian at Mesa Public Library in Mesa, Arizona. She has been working with young adult volunteers for six years and is a reviewer for **VOYA***.*

Appendix B

PUBLIC LIBRARY
YA Program RoundUp

"KidWorks Is Kid-Made":

A Teen Volunteer Program That Won't Quit

Kathy MacMillan

A young attendee shows off her craft at KidsWorks Presents: Spring Fling.

WHAT: KidWorks
WHERE: Eldersburg Branch of the Carroll County Public Library in Eldersburg, Maryland
WHO: Up to thirty children and teens each month, ages nine and up
WHEN: The second and fourth Thursday of each month
HOW: To present monthly library programs for younger children, KidWorks meets twice a month, once for planning and once for the presentation, which is open to the public. Middle and high school students earn service-learning hours as KidWorks members. Each month's program is separate; members commit to only two meetings at a time.

Back in 1999, our library had a great tradition of programming for grades one to three, but we also wanted to attract older youth. We set out to create a program that would meet our community's specific needs while providing a fun time for teens. First, we came up with the basic outline. Group members would not have to come every month, the only requirement being to attend two meetings during the same month. Each month's programming would be self-contained.

Then we asked what would work for the teens. After we advertised in the branch and at local schools, 31 young people attended our kickoff informational meeting in September 1999. We explained the group's concept, and participants voted on when to meet (Thursdays from 5:30 to 7:30 p.m.), the group's name, and program topics for the first several months.

They chose the name "KidWorks" because it reflects what the group is all about. Although a librarian facilitates meetings and provides guidance, the teens themselves come up with the ideas, vote on program contents, and present the programs. In the words of group member Jessica Geyer, "KidWorks is kid-made."

The bulk of the work is actually done within the children's program itself. A typical month of KidWorks follows a pattern of activities during two meetings.

Before Meeting #1

The librarian prepares the sign-in sheet, name tags, an icebreaker, and several book and craft ideas to jump-start the brainstorming process.

Meeting #1 (Planning)

1. **Registration:** Participants make name tags and sign in (indicating whether or not they are earning service hours).
2. **Introductions:** We go around the room to introduce ourselves. Each person answers the silly question of the month, such as "What color is your toothbrush?" This opening creates a friendly atmosphere quickly.
3. **Icebreaker:** Short, fun games encourage teamwork and help participants get to know one another (KidWorks members call it "the corny game").
4. **Ground rules/Introduction:** The librarian reviews the KidWorks process and introduces the month's topic. (The

group chooses topics quarterly to accommodate our publicity schedule.) We go over things to remember, such as how our materials are limited to what we can make or find in the library, and that our activities must be appropriate for young children.

5. **Brainstorm list of activities:** Using a chalkboard, we list ideas as people think of them. Group members take turns writing on the board—middle schoolers love being "teacher"!
6. **Group vote:** Group members vote for as many ideas as they like.
7. **Pull out top choices and plan program format:** The librarian's guidance comes into play, making suggestions for program flow.
8. **Assign roles for program:** On the board, we list all the "jobs" in the program. Some jobs can be divided into multiple tasks (for example, if we will read a book in the program, one person reads the story while another shows the pictures). Then we fill the roles by using KidWorks' trademark number system: Everyone who wants a particular job stands up. The librarian chooses a number and whispers it to one of the sitting members. Each standing member guesses a number, and whoever guesses closest wins the job. It's a fast and fair way to assign roles, and it avoids complaints.
9. **Prepare materials:** Make a list of items to find or make. Break into groups to prepare crafts, construct skits, practice stories, etc.
10. **Rehearse:** Run through the program (if time allows).
11. **Publicity flyers:** The librarian reminds the group about the next meeting time and hands out flyers for the program they will present. KidWorks members are encouraged to distribute flyers to family and friends.

Our very first program, KidWorks Presents: Halloween Fun

PHOTO CREDITS: Debby Parker

KidWorks Presents: March Magic

BETWEEN MEETINGS #1 AND #2

The librarian makes name tags for the group members, fills out service-hour forms, and gathers materials needed for the program.

MEETING #2

1. Complete name tags and sign-in.
2. Go over the program structure and assignments.
3. Set up the room and finish preparations.
4. Run through the program.
5. Group members greet program attendees in the Children's Department and make name tags for them from 6:20 to 6:30 p.m.
6. The program presentation begins at 6:30 p.m.
7. The program ends at approximately 7:15 p.m.; group members clean up the room.
8. The librarian hands out service-hour forms and reminds the group about next month's meeting dates and topic.

GETTING POPULAR

KidWorks has attracted more than two hundred different participants since it began in September 1999. Some have come once or twice, and many have returned month after month. We promote the program when we visit local schools and run our annual Volunteer Fair. Those who do not get into our volunteer program receive a flyer inviting them to try KidWorks. Average monthly attendance is twelve teens; in recent months we have had the problem of *too many* teens showing up to participate in KidWorks. As a result, we are in the process of starting a second group on Wednesday nights, with participation in each group limited to the first fifteen people who arrive.

SURFIN' THE JUKEBOX

KidWorks presentations have included a Magic Show, Zany Zoo, Talent Show, Dance Dance Dance, Face Painting Fun, Crazy Crafts, Story Jukebox, Kids' Karaoke, Sand Art, Castle Capers, USA Day, and more.

KidWorks members prepare crafts for the Spring Fling program.

The Story Jukebox is one of our most successful and creative programs. Twelve participants divide into pairs, each pair picking a topic such as Baby Books or Animal Books. Then each pair makes a "jukebox" out of posterboard, with five slots for coins and a space for a picture next to each slot. Choosing five books relating to their topic, teams paste pictures of the book covers on the jukebox beside the slots. When the smaller children arrive for the program, each receives a handful of "story coins" to spend at the various jukeboxes around the room. Each child goes to the jukebox of her choice, selects a story, and drops in a coin. Then a KidWorks member pops out from behind the jukebox to read the book aloud. We have offered the Story Jukebox several times, and it is always a hit.

More typical is a program such as the Surfing Party, presented this past June. It consisted of the

Vanessa and Heather perform a flute duet at KidWorks Presents: Talent Show.

read-aloud story, **Mrs. Armitage and the Big Wave** by Quentin Black (Harcourt, 1998), a round of "Surfer Dude Says" ("Simon Says"), a lip-sync performance of the Beach Boys' "Surfin' USA" by KidWorks members, the Limbo, and a beach-scene postcard craft. Our programs tend to follow this format, beginning with a book and ending with a craft, with lots of interactive activities in between.

Although we have never had a program that fell completely flat—that's the beauty of preteen and young teen energy—there have been some problematic elements. Because of our indoor space and wide age range of attendees, we stopped offering complicated events such as relay races and competitive games. Even more so than in conventional library story times, we must make sure that stories are short, catchy, and interactive; otherwise we risk losing the attention of both the older and younger portions of the audience.

WHY KIDWORKS WORKS

- **It addresses the needs of our community:** Eldersburg has a huge demand for service-hour opportunities. KidWorks also meets the teens' need for short-term commitments and flexible scheduling. It draws fourth and fifth graders into the library, keeping them interested when they enter middle school by offering service-hours. Because it involves active participation and a quick payoff for their efforts, it shows young people what they can do.
- **Flexibility:** The schedule of meetings is flexible enough to fit around other commitments. KidWorks members simply skip the months when they have soccer or dance recitals. We keep the publicity in the flyers vague enough so that participants can contribute their own ideas around the theme each month. In addition, such publicity allows the librarian to do a program alone in the unlikely event that no KidWorks members show up.
- **Attitude:** From the beginning, KidWorks has been about the young people themselves. It can be difficult for the librarian to back off and let them run the show, but that's what we have to do. It's not always perfect, but it is usually creative and always full of heart! The librarian's role in this program is as a guide, not a dictator.

COMMENTS FROM TEENS AND PARENTS

"It's a wonderful experience and a great way to earn service hours. If you're someone who is shy, it doesn't matter."—Jessica Geyer, age 13.

"I have been doing KidWorks since I was 9 years old. Back when I started, I couldn't even get service hours, but I wanted to do it anyway. Also, when I was 10 and 11, I had my arm in a brace or cast much of the time. Miss Kathy always found something I could do, so I wasn't left out. I have always loved KidWorks and will continue to do it as long as I can."—Andy Cobun, age 12.

"[KidWorks] is a great opportunity for kids to work together to make something happen and to make a difference. They do the planning and the work, and make the mistakes, and together they create a product that is fun and that benefits the community. They learn that they can make decisions, and that someone will actually take their opinions seriously!"—Nancy Bobby, KidWorks parent.

Kathy MacMillan works part-time as a children's librarian at the Eldersburg Branch of Carroll County Public Library in Eldersburg, Maryland. She is also the librarian at Maryland School for the Deaf in Columbia, Maryland. Her first **VOYA** *article was* A Flood of Tears: Titanic and the Tearjerker Romance *in February 1999, when she was Kathleen M. Kelly.*

Kellie M. Gillespie has written a column reviewing websites for teens in *Voice of Youth Advocates* (*VOYA*) called "YA Clicks" and is author of the *VOYA* article "Top Ten Myths and Realities of Working with Teen Volunteers" (as Kellie Shoemaker, April 1998). In addition, she has co-authored an article about using the Internet for student research that appeared in *Resources in Education* as part of the Education Resources Information Center (ERIC) database. She is a member of the American Library Association and the Arizona Library Association.

She has worked as a children's, young adult, and adult services librarian and is now a fiction specialist for the City of Mesa Library in Mesa, Arizona. She has worked with teen volunteers for more than ten years in a variety of programs, including summer reading, crafts, storytelling, poetry contests, reading buddies, and teen services in general. Her experience with teen volunteers includes developing innovative programs such as *FRANK Magazine*, a literary magazine by and for teens with a volunteer editorial board that was recognized as one of the nation's top teen library programs in *Excellence in Library Services to Young Adults* (1997).

Gillespie lives in Chandler, Arizona, with her husband and her two youngest children, who are both in their teens. She would like to thank all four of her children for contributing so much material to this book, even if they didn't know it at the time and would be totally embarrassed if they ever read it. This is her first book.